MW01007766

The Magic of Shabbos

A Journey Through the Shabbos Experience

By

Rabbi Mordechai Rhine

© Copyright 1998 by Rabbi Mordechai Rhine

ALL RIGHTS RESERVED.
NO PART OF THIS BOOK MAY BE REPRODUCED
OR TRANSMITTED IN ANY FORM OR BY ANY MEANS
(ELECTRONIC, PHOTOCOPYING, RECORDING
OR OTHERWISE) WITHOUT PRIOR WRITTEN
PERMISSION OF THE PUBLISHER.

ISBN 1-880582-25-2 (hardbound)
ISBN 1-880582-26-0 (softbound)

THE JUDAICA PRESS, INC.
123 Ditmas Avenue
Brooklyn, New York 11218
718-972-6200   800-972-6201
JudaicaPr@aol.com

Manufactured in the United States of America

"Those who taste it
have tasted life.
Those who love its words
have chosen greatness."

(From the Shabbos prayers.)

בס״ד   מכתב ברכה

       The Psalmist sings out "Taste and see that G-d is good." It is unfortunate that many of our brethern have not had the opportunity to taste in order to see.

       Rav Mordechai Rhine ''ג has therefore decided to influence those who have not yet tasted to see firstly in order that they eventually taste. By sharing his feelings about Shabbos with others, by writing about its many laws and customs, by relating inspiring stories, even by translating the Zmiros, he inculcates a strong desire to become a participant in a major precept of Judaism.

       More power to him. May he go from strength to strength in his kiruv endeavors.

                           Rabbi David Cohen
                           6 Marcheshvan 5798

ISRAEL MEIR LAU
Chief Rabbi of Israel

ישראל מאיר לאו
הרב הראשי לישראל

20 Elul 5757
September 30, 1997
R-63-97

Rabbi Mordecai Rhine
7 Waverly Place
Monsey, NY 10952
USA

Dear Rabbi Mordecai Rhine:

The book "The Magic of Shabbos" is an essential handbook explaining in depth the holiness of Shabbos. It integrates philosophical ideas, traditional values and a precise explanation of the Shabbos laws.

This primer will surely be of great assistance to those seeking to enjoy the serenity of the holy Shabbos day, and will play an important role in building and strengthening the American Jewish community.

Wishing much Hatzlacha and a Shana Tovah.

Sincerely Yours,

Israel Meir Lau
Chief Rabbi of Israel

בית יהב, ירמיהו 80, ירושלים, ת.ד. 7525 טל. 02-5313191 פקס. 02-5377872
Beit Yahav, 80 Yirmiyahu St., Jerusalem P.O.B. 7525 Tel. 02-5313191 Fax. 02-5377872

Beth Medrash Govoha

Rabbi Aaron Kotler Institute for Advanced Learning
617 Sixth Street, Lakewood, NJ 08701 • (908)367-1060
Fax:(908)367-7487

November 3, 1997

Mordechai Y. Rhine
7 Waverly Place
Monsey, NY 10952

Dear Mordechai,

I was pleased to see your inspirational work about Shabbos, explaining the essence of Shabbos in an uplifting manner. Our sages have emphasized the role of Shabbos as a unifying force of the Jewish people. I have confidence that this wonderful book will foster good will throughout the Jewish world.

With pleasure,

Rabbi Yeruchem Olshin
Rosh Yeshiva

הרב דוב בערל ווין
Rabbi Berel Wein
12 Hilltop Place
Monsey, New York 10952

_____

(914) 425-5919

May 12, 1997

Mordechai Rhine
7 Waverly Place
Monsey, N.Y. 10952

Dear Mordechai,

I have read your wonderful work on "The Magic of Shabbos". Its name truly implies the magic quality of your book which will be of immense help to any Jew seeking to enjoy the serenity and holiness of Shabbos. You have combined philosophical ideas, traditional values, clear and precise halacha with practical suggestions for Sabbath observance that make this book an essential primer for all those seeking Shabbos in their lives. I am certain that this book will be of great consequence and will play an important role in helping build the American Jewish Community.

Sincerely yours,

Rabbi Berel Wein

Table of Contents

Preface xi
Acknowledgments. xiv
Foreword. xvii
A Note to the Reader xvii
Dedication xix
Introduction xxi

The Day of Shabbos

1. Preparing for the Queen 1
2. Candle-lighting 6
3. The Source of Blessing 12
4. Friday Night 19
5. Shabbos Morning 36
6. Shabbos Lunch 43
7. Shabbos Afternoon 60
8. Spiritual Growth 67
9. *Havdalah*, Bidding Farewell. 70

The Laws of Shabbos

Introduction 79
10. Jewish Law—The Basics 85

11. A Definition of Working 92
12. The Thirty-Nine Categories/Gardening 98
13. Food Preparation 103
14. Cloth Production 111
15. Leather Production 116
16. Miscellaneous Categories 121
17. Erecting the Sanctuary 128
18. Muktza 134
19. On Jewish Continuity 142
20. In Conclusion 145
21. Opportunities For Study 147
22. Shabbos Recipes 158
23. Questions and Answers 162
Endnotes 171
Glossary 181
Index 185
Bibliography 189

Preface

It is with great gratitude to G-d that I set out to write this manuscript. "For He has sustained me to reach this day," to have the opportunity not only to learn myself, but also, to share that learning with others.

To my grandparents on both sides goes a special debt of gratitude. Their respective sacrifices for Shabbos during difficult times have been an inspiration to me. Particular thanks to my mother's father, my namesake, to whom this book is dedicated. Additionally, a special "Thank You" to Zeide and Savtie for hosting me during a wonderful week in Jerusalem.

My beloved parents are probably the hardest ones to thank. How can I thank the people who raised and nurtured me—both physically and spiritually? They encouraged me and supported me year after year. Their dedication to Jewish education is the cause to which I attribute my Torah learning.

But greater than their general commitment to Judaism, I must thank my parents for making Torah relevant to me. Torah generally, and Shabbos in particular, were never "family heirlooms" thrust upon me. They were not "Daddy's day off," in which we participated. Instead, they were mine. It is my Shabbos, as it is the Shabbos of every Jew. I hope that this book will help convey this message.

"And a teacher brings the student to eternal life." How do I thank the Rabbis who guided me in my Torah learning? How do I thank my Rabbis for the eternal gift of loving Torah? I pray that they may all see much joy from their children and students. May G-d bless them for their tremendous dedication.

To my Rebbe, Rabbi Berel Wein, goes a special note of appreciation. Perhaps Rebbe's greatest trait is that he doesn't lose faith in his students. It was like that in yeshiva; when we turned the place upside down, he waited patiently. Success was always the product of a lot of effort and a lot of patience. I believe it is like that in the Jewish world as well. May G-d bless us that his faith and patience will find fruition, "So that no Jew will be pushed away" or be left behind. May we live to see the day when there will be no Jew—from one end of the country to the other—who isn't fluent in the laws of Torah, and in the joys of being Jewish.

To all my friends who encouraged me through challenging decisions: Thank You. To my brother Yonoson Boruch, who convinced me that it was worth the effort; to my study partner Rabbi Pinchas Juravel, who proofread the original draft and convinced me that it could be done; to Chaim and Aliza for their optimism, and to the Weissmans for being the wonderful people they are. Also, many thanks to Rabbi Yitzchok Heimowitz, Rabbi Yanky and Mrs. Oppen, Yisroel Epstein and Zeide for their incisive comments and assistance. May we share good tidings with one another, and blessings with all of Israel.

I pray that G-d enable me to build a proper Jewish home—a home dedicated to Torah and to the principles that the Shabbos personifies. May we all continue to build and contribute to the Jewish world, as we constantly strive towards peace, toward the ultimate fulfillment of creation. May we "go from strength to strength, until such time that we once again present ourselves before G-d in Zion." May it be rebuilt speedily and in our days. Amen.

July 22, 1996
The sixth day of Av,
the month that will be changed to one of rejoicing.
The holy city of Jerusalem,
at the Western Wall.

Acknowledgments

My dearest thanks to Rabbi and Mrs. Gruman for hosting me for many a wonderful Shabbos in Twin Rivers, New Jersey. Many of the stories and insights are based on my experiences in their home. I can think of no friendlier starting point than the Twin Rivers community and Shalom Torah Centers.

Words cannot express my appreciation to my parents for their assistance during the difficult phases of writing this book. Many thanks to my *kallah*, Yittie, for her understanding and encouragement. To my future parents-in-law, Mr. and Mrs. Schaum, I express my thanks and the hope that the home that Yittie and I set out to build should be a source of pride to our parents and all of Israel.

Many thanks to the staff at The Judaica Press for their efficiency and devotion to this project. The editors, Bonnie Goldman and Elinor Nauen, have done a super job editing the manuscript. Thanks also to Yehudis Friedman for championing my book and for her excellent proofreading and to Zisi Berkowitz for her elegant book design and formatting work. They all worked on the manuscript with unusual sensitivity, and have produced a inspirational and enjoyable book.

My sincere appreciation to the many people who proofread the manuscript and offered their encouragement and insightful comments. Among them: Rabbi J. Fischer, Ari Gertz, Rabbi

Reuven Green, Scott Kalchstein, Susan Lesser, Moish Miller, Rabbi Yitzchak Rosenbaum and the staff at NJOP, Rabbi A.J. Rosenberg, Rabbi Yehudah Schwab, Rabbi and Mrs. Yakov Shulman, Rabbi Moshe Travitsky, Craig Tuz, Naftoli Walfish, Rabbi and Mrs. Michoel Yardly, and Yoni.

Growing up in a yeshiva I learned many things, and the words of my Rebbe echo clearly in my mind. "Boys," he said, "it is a rough world. But if you stay connected to a yeshiva, you'll be okay." I am eternally grateful for that advice, and thankful for the yeshivohs in which I learned.

Special appreciation to the Roshei Yeshiva of Beth Medrash Govoha in Lakewood, New Jersey, for their dedication to the yeshiva. Words cannot describe the joy of entering a study hall filled with Torah study. Also, tremendous appreciation to my study partners and friends whose encouragement, patience and advice made this book possible. Among them: Rabbis Abba Moshe Barer, Nesanel Berkowitz, Tzvi Goldman, Yitzchok Gronstein, Dovid Irons, Pinchas Juravel, Eliyahu Lopian, Chagai Yom Tov Matzliach, Yaakov Rosenblatt, Shimon Rosenblum, Chanoch Saltz, Elly Selengut, Ushi Smith, Dov Wachman and Mordechai Weichbrod.

During the writing and editing process I had the good fortune to consult with many Rabbis whose guidance, patience and advice are most appreciated. Among them: Rabbi Simcha Bunim Cohen, both in person and through his wonderful books, Rabbi Shmuel Felder, Rabbi Yaacov Haber, Rabbi Yoel Kramer, Rabbi Yacov Lipschutz, Rabbi Dr. Shimon Russell, Rabbi Chaim Pinchas Scheinberg, Rabbi Chaim Schwartz, Mr.

Avi Shulman, and Rabbis Berel and Chaim Wein.

Finally, and most importantly, I thank G-d, "Who placed my lot among those dedicated to Torah. For we run and others run; we run to eternal life."

May G-d sweeten His Torah in our mouths and in the mouths of the entire Jewish people. May we, and all our descendants be knowledgeable in Torah and in the sweetness of Jewish observance.

The Ninth of Cheshvan,
November 9, 1997
Monsey, New York

Foreword

About three years ago, at a Shabbos table in Twin Rivers, New Jersey, I was challenged to explain the purpose of Shabbos and its intricate laws. Realizing that I didn't understand Shabbos nearly as well as I should, I accepted the challenge.

I studied the laws; I observed the Shabbos table. The more I learned about it, the more I came to appreciate and love it. I found that Shabbos speaks to the Jew, logically as well as emotionally. I discovered that there is a magical, hidden quality to Shabbos. It is that magic of Shabbos that I wish to share with you.

A Note to the Reader

This book is intended to introduce the beauty of Shabbos. It is most useful as a starting point, as a tool for spiritual growth.

Perhaps you've yearned to know more about the meaning of candle-lighting or how to recite kiddush. Or you've wondered what exactly happens in the synagogue service and why. Each section is devoted to one aspect of the Shabbos experience and will guide you through it one step at a time.

If you've been confused by the many Shabbos laws, the chapters explaining them will be most helpful. Study these sections at your own pace, and you will gradually perceive the Divine system that makes this day so special.

From start to finish this book is dedicated to the wonders of
Shabbos. No matter what level of observance you are accus-
tomed to, this book will assist you in bringing the joy of
Shabbos into your life.

Dedication

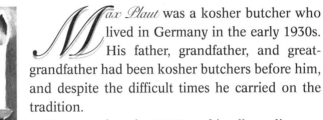

Max Plaut was a kosher butcher who lived in Germany in the early 1930s. His father, grandfather, and great-grandfather had been kosher butchers before him, and despite the difficult times he carried on the tradition.

One evening, in 1935, a friendly policeman whispered to him, "You're on the list for tomorrow." Nothing more need be said. After such a warning, the Nazi threat was too real to be ignored. That night, Max fled Germany with his wife and two children, and they eventually arrived in the land of Israel. There, Max worked as part of a road repair crew, building and repairing roads near his Haifa home. Sometimes, the sun would beat down brutally for many hours, leaving sunburn marks where his tattered clothes did not cover his skin.

After some time, he managed to establish a butcher store on the ground floor of his new home. There he spent his days selling meat to the local families.

One Shabbos, the electricity went out. As Max sat at his Shabbos table, singing the Shabbos songs, some concerned neighbors came to visit him. "Aren't you going to check on your meat?" they asked. "Perhaps there is something to be done to keep the meat from spoiling."

Max wouldn't hear of it. "I left Germany with next to nothing, and I still have very little. But my Shabbos is still mine. Even if every piece of meat rots, I will not go into that store on *my* Shabbos."

Max's commitment to Shabbos left an indelible message on his family, a message that lives on in the hearts of his children and grandchildren. It is to his memory, my grandfather and namesake, that I dedicate this book.

Introduction

Barry is a traveling salesman and a devoutly religious Jew. He is always careful to get to his Shabbos destination with plenty of time to spare. He expected to reach his cousins in Dallas, Texas by two o'clock Friday afternoon. But unforeseen difficulties were headed his way.

As Barry entered Interstate 20, he was astonished. It seemed as if every car in the state of Texas had converged on this one highway. Barry patiently "stopped and went" with the traffic flow, but by three he realized that he simply wasn't going to make it to his destination in time for Shabbos. As he sat in traffic, panic gripped him. Questions began to race through his mind. What would he do for Shabbos? Where would he sleep? Where would he eat? He realized that he had to take action.

He pulled off the highway into a nameless town and searched for accommodations. He passed a few deserted cottages and continued as he saw nothing but open fields and grazing cattle. Still looking for a sign of friendly civilization, he drove on, until he arrived at a police station. The desk sergeant couldn't grant him ideal accommodations, "But if you want, we do have a prison, and you can sleep there if you'd like."

Barry happily accepted.

It didn't take long for the inmates to start "friendly" conversation with him. "I'm here for armed robbery, and they gave me a ten year sentence."

"And I'm here for murdering my girlfriend's father; they gave me seven years."

Suddenly, their attention turned to Barry. "And what are you here for?" they asked.

"Shabbos," was Barry's response.

"And what do you get for *that?*"

"Life," was Barry's soft reply.

Indeed, Shabbos is one of the most important aspects of Jewish life. It is through Shabbos that we achieve life's true blessings. Shabbos endows us with an appreciation for life in a physical, emotional and psychological sense. A home that knows the joy of Shabbos will appreciate the grandeur of the Jewish people.

Shabbos is a special day designated to discovering our personal role in creation. It gives us the opportunity to explore our inner strengths and to appreciate the blessings of life. Additionally, Shabbos gives us quality time with the people we care about—our family and friends—and helps these relationships grow richer.

Herman Wouk, a noted author, playwright, and a religious Jew describes what Shabbos means to him, to his family, and to our nation. In *This is My G-d* he writes:

"Leaving the gloomy theater, the littered coffee cups, the jumbled scarred-up scripts, the haggard actors, the shouting stagehands, the bedeviled director, the knuckle-gnawing producer, the clattering typewriter, and the dense tobacco smoke and backstage dust, I have come home. It has been a startling change, very like a brief return from the wars. My wife and my boys, whose existence I have almost forgotten in the anxious shoring up of the tottering ruin, are waiting for me, gay, dressed in holiday clothes, and looking to me marvelously attractive..."

Wouk goes on to describe the beauty of his Shabbos meal. He writes:

"...We have sat down to a splendid dinner, at a table graced with flowers and the old Sabbath symbols: the burning candles, the twisted loaves, the stuffed fish and my grandfather's silver goblet brimming with wine. I have blessed my boys with the ancient blessing; we have sung the pleasantly syncopated Sabbath table hymns. The talk has little to do with tottering ruins. My wife and I have caught up with our week's conversation. The boys, knowing that the Sabbath is the occasion for asking questions, have asked them. The Bible, the encyclopedia, the atlas, have piled up on the table. We talk of Judaism, and there are the usual impossible boys' queries about G-d, which my wife and I field clumsily but as well as we can. For me it is a retreat into restorative magic."[1]

Throughout the centuries, Shabbos observance has been challenged by the nations of the world. As early as the Greek empire (167 BCE), anti-Shabbos laws were legislated to prevent its observance. But Jews never wavered in their commitment to Shabbos.

Shabbos symbolizes the perseverance of the Jewish people and the Jewish link to eternity. Shabbos can grant us a new perspective on life, a serenity and an appreciation of who we are, and what kind of people we would like to become.

Spain was a scary place for a Jew to be in 1492. As Columbus set sail to discover a land of religious tolerance, Christian Spain began its infamous Inquisition. Aided by its dreaded secret police, the Hermandad, the Inquisition sought to kill the Jews.

During this time Don Manuel Elfradi was a secret Jew who learned to keep to himself his true allegiances. His ancestors had come to Spain 400 years earlier, fleeing religious persecution. And now, at least to the outside world, the Elfradi family had become Christians.

There was a limit to how long they could pretend allegiance to Christianity. Although they lived in a small town, they feared they would be found out and the Hermandad would pay them a visit. They lived in daily dread, knowing that one fateful visit could expose the fact that Don Manuel was secretly raising his children as Jews.

A decision had to be made. To relocate to Holland, a land of religious tolerance, was simply not an option. He was not wealthy enough for that. But to abdicate his position as a Jewish father, responsible for the next link of Jewish legacy, was equally unthinkable. Finally, he hit upon a solution.

In the dead of night, Don Manuel began to dig an underground room to meet his family's religious needs. It took months to construct, and it was small, but it served the purpose well. Here he stored his religious books and educated his children in the ways of his people. In this little room he taught them of the covenant of old, and of the dedication of their parents to that great legacy.

Don Manuel's children grew up as secret Jews; as adults, they decided that they no longer wished to live a double life. With perseverance they relocated to Holland, where they re-founded the family on friendlier soil. Today, five centuries later, a number of Don Manuel's descendants can be found living on a side street in Tel Aviv. They speak of an ancestor of long ago, whose dedication to Judaism kept their family alive. Every Friday night they sing a haunting melody that they say was authored by Don Manuel himself, in his secret room. As they sing, they remember that courageous decision of his, a decision of dedication and commitment which reaps dividends to our very day.

But there is no need to search the history books for stories of Jewish courage. Commitment to Shabbos is alive and well today.

One such story occurred recently in a popular religious girls' summer camp where Leah is the head counselor. Known for her exuberance and her ability to take charge, Leah's loving personality has endeared her to the campers.

Leah had invited a group of girls to visit the camp for Shabbos. These girls were from traditional homes, but had never experienced the complete observance of Shabbos. They had recently decided they wanted to know more. Leah felt that Shabbos in a camp atmosphere would be an enjoyable experience, and would give them an opportunity to see the richness of Shabbos from a closer perspective. They would experience the way Shabbos is spent in summer camp—a day replete with songs, games, and a relaxed atmosphere. But here it was, the sun was setting, it was time for lighting the Shabbos candles, and the girls had still not arrived.

Leah was worried. Had the girls run into traffic? Maybe they had changed their minds about coming? As doubt gnawed at Leah, she led the Friday night meal with her usual exuberance, all the while wondering about her friends who did not show up.

Some say it was 9:00 p.m., others say it was 9:30 p.m., when the missing girls finally appeared. They pranced into the dining room, a tired but smiling group; they were looking for Leah. "You see," they explained breathlessly, "We were still on the road when we realized that sunset had arrived. We pulled the car over, and decided to walk; we weren't going to drive on Shabbos! It took us a while to walk the remaining four miles, but we're so glad that we did!"

It didn't take long for the campers to happily serve a second Shabbos meal. That meal was indeed "fit for a queen." For it was a special meal, honoring the dedication of those Daughters of Israel who had so steadfastly expressed their commitment to the treasure called Shabbos.

Not only is Shabbos special in a spiritual sense. Even in a physical sense, Shabbos is a magnificent treasure.

The story is told of a doctor who said that she had been keeping Shabbos "two years before I believed in G-d!"

When the listeners expressed astonishment, she explained. "I saw how Shabbos cared for the emotional and physical needs of a human being. I saw the warmth and happiness that it generated in the Jewish home. I was committed not to let my belief or lack thereof, stand in the way of my enjoying its benefits."

Although there are many magnificent parts of Jewish life, Shabbos is a precious gem. Many an outsider has seen this concept clearly. As Herman Wouk recounts: "My producer one Saturday night said to me, 'I don't envy you your religion, but I envy you your Sabbath.' " [2]

What is it about Shabbos that generates such enthusiasm and dedication? And how does the Shabbos relate to us in our modern times?

These are questions which we will discuss and explore in the coming chapters.

◆ ◆ ◆

How many days did it take for G-d to create the world? "Six," you say. Try again. "Seven?" Not quite. Let me explain.

It is well known that G-d "created the world in six days, and on the seventh day He rested." [3] Nevertheless, the Torah clearly tells us (Genesis 2:2), "And G-d completed, on the seventh day, the work that He had done." If G-d, in fact, completed His work on the seventh day, that would imply that some sort of creation was done on the holy day of Shabbos!

Rashi, an eleventh century Biblical scholar from France, explains this apparent contradiction by telling us: Indeed all of creation was done in six days. Nevertheless, something was still missing. After six days of creation, what was the world still missing? Rest. With Shabbos, the concept of rest was introduced. Through it, creation was completed.

In other words, G-d *did* create something on the seventh day, but He did so without doing any "work". On the seventh day, G-d created the concept of "rest," or in Hebrew, *menucha*. What exactly is this great concept of rest or *menucha*, that it is considered the crowning glory of creation?

It is understood that every person wants to be happy. Many people feel that money will bring happiness, while others look to having a wide circle of admirers. Some spend their lives saving for their old age, looking toward retirement as a time of rest and happiness. Alas, despite their efforts, many people, even after they have achieved great success, are left with a void, a feeling of emptiness.

The common theme of these approaches is that they address only our physical dimension. In reality, it is our soul that craves fulfillment. Our internal self—our spiritual dimension—is the part of us that feels empty. By refocusing our goals towards spirituality, it is possible to find meaning in life.

Judaism approaches the search for happiness from a unique perspective. Certainly, we should work for the betterment of society and strive to improve our lot. But Judaism recognizes that, ultimately, true happiness comes from within. Our Rabbis taught, "Who is wealthy? He who is happy with his lot."[4] By reassessing our values, we can achieve true happiness.

This is the focus of Shabbos. Six days a week we strive to improve our lot, to enhance our lives and the lives of those around us. On Shabbos we change our focus. Instead of striving to develop our physical dimension, we emphasize the development of our inner strength, in an effort to become better human beings. On Shabbos we nurture and develop ourselves in an intellectual and spiritual sense. The focus of Shabbos helps us recognize that it is neither our popularity nor the size of our bank account that can give us true fulfillment. It is through our families and our spiritual goals that we will be able to achieve self-fulfillment. Through this recognition, true happiness can be achieved.[5]

This concept of striving for a higher spiritual goal explains why we refrain from various actions on Shabbos. In essence, as we prepare for Shabbos we are saying, "We must take care of these actions before Shabbos, because on Shabbos we are occupied with a higher mission." Everything must be completed before Shabbos, so that on Shabbos we will not be distracted.

Shabbos, and the rest or *menucha* it brings, is far more than just physical rest. *Menucha* represents fulfillment, in a physical, spiritual, and emotional sense. Shabbos provides the opportunity to discover the happiness and harmony for which we strive. Shabbos affords us the opportunity to rest from our hectic lives and enjoy G-d's Creation. Through the gift of Shabbos G-d shows us how a Jew can find fulfillment in life.

Many people view the laws of Shabbos as restrictive. However, the laws of Shabbos do not restrict; they guide. Within the discipline of these laws we are shown how to experience spiritual greatness. By avoiding certain distractions, we can find serenity.

Unfortunately, many Jews do not understand the positive sense of the Shabbos laws. In this book the deeper meanings of some of these laws will be explained in order to help you appreciate Shabbos in its most positive sense.

There is an ancient legend that when the dove was created, it was created without wings. The dove was attacked by the other animals and pleaded to G-d for help. G-d heard the dove's prayer, and graced it with a glorious set of wings. Soon the dove complained bitterly to G-d. "Things were bad enough before You placed these cumbersome limbs on my sides. But at least I was able to run from my enemies. Now with these wings, I am weighed down, and I can't even run properly."

G-d smiled benevolently upon the dove, and said, "Come, I will show you how to use your wings to fly. In this way, you will never view your wings as a burden, but rather as the special gift they were meant to be."

Similarly, our sages teach us that the commandments of the Torah are compared to a pair of wings.[6] Until we learn to use them, they may weigh us down. But once we learn how to use them properly, they give us the ability to "fly"—to inspire us and to bring light into our hearts and homes.

Let us therefore investigate Shabbos about which G-d told Moses, "There is a special treasure in My treasure house, and its name is Shabbos; I would like to give it to the Jewish people. Go, and tell them..."[7]

♦ ♦ ♦

The Medrash (Leviticus 9:3) tells us that the eminent Talmudic sage Rabbi Yanai once invited a distinguished looking Jew to his home. After allowing the man to eat to his heart's content, Rabbi Yanai asked him to say a Torah thought. The man repeatedly declined Rabbi Yanai's request, and it eventually became clear that the man did not know Torah. Struck by this fact, Rabbi Yanai became depressed, as he reflected upon this unfortunate situation.

Suddenly the man arose and began to berate Rabbi Yanai, "Thief! Thief! You have stolen my inheritance."

Rabbi Yanai was shocked by this outburst. The man explained, "I once passed by a school for Jewish children, and I heard their teacher state, 'Torah was commanded to us through Moses, as an inheritance to the House of Jacob.'[8] It is not written 'An inheritance to the House of Yanai,' but rather, 'an inheritance to the House of Jacob.' As a descendent of our forefather Jacob, I, too, have a right to that inheritance. It is you, the Talmudic sage, who have deprived me of my inheritance. Instead of getting upset over how little I know, it is your responsibility to teach me! In that way you will restore the inheritance to its rightful owner!"

In our generation, there are many Jews who have never had the opportunity to learn Torah. For various reasons, thousands of Jews have been deprived of their heritage. Let us therefore discuss the details of Shabbos. In this way, with G-d's help, it will once again become the inheritance of the entire House of Jacob, the rightful pride of every Jew.

Let us recognize that Shabbos observance may require some effort and change, but then again, as you know, that is true for any good, healthy relationship. Just as our relationship with our parents, children and spouse require constant effort, so, too, our relationship with Shabbos requires attention and constant effort.

Also, just as any strong relationship will reap dividends well beyond our efforts, so will the Shabbos be a source of blessing to us—beyond all expectations. Then we will recognize Shabbos as the personal treasure of the Jewish people—a treasure that belongs to, and should be cherished by, every one of us.

With this goal in mind, I have balanced this book to cover many interests. Stories, songs, observances, and explanations blend together to create the mosaic of a pleasurable Shabbos experience. This book will guide you through the day of Shabbos, with "how to do it" sections throughout. Relax and enjoy as we explore the meaning of Shabbos and why its observance has been so dear to the Jewish people for such a long time. Shabbos is much more than the seventh day of the week. To the observant Jew, Shabbos is a link to eternity.

Preparing for the Queen

Shabbos is aptly referred to as the Shabbos Queen. Our relationship to Shabbos is like a relationship with a spouse —like a marriage. With the advent of Shabbos we become royalty. We dress in our finest garments as we welcome our bride, the Shabbos Queen.

The Talmud tells us, "He who toils before Shabbos shall eat on Shabbos."[1] While this is certainly a practical piece of wisdom, it also contains a dynamic insight into the way we, as Jews, lead our lives. The entire week is seen as a preparation for Shabbos. Shabbos is the day of inspiration, the climax of the entire week. We prepare for it expectantly, knowing that the more involved we are in its preparations, the more we will appreciate the beauty of the day.

All preparations for Shabbos are considered an honor. The Talmud (Shabbos 119a) relates how the noble Rav Yosef would chop wood to stoke the fire before Shabbos began. The most mundane tasks take on an aura of holiness when they are done to honor Shabbos. This includes cleaning the table, vacuuming, polishing the shoes, and, yes, even taking out the garbage.

Preparations for Shabbos take place all week. If, for example, while shopping, you notice a particular delicacy, you might buy it and save it for Shabbos. Also, everyone in the family should have chores to do in honor of Shabbos. If you have children, get them involved in the excitement. Plan the necessary jobs well in advance so that they can help you with the preparations.

Try to get home early on Friday afternoon to involve yourself with the preparations. It is said that the great Rabbi Epstein of Novardok (1829-1908, Lithuania) used to encourage people to close their businesses early on Friday afternoon. He once commented, "When I get to Heaven, they will ask me what I have done during my lifetime. I will not respond by telling them about the books I have written, or the community I have led. Rather, I will tell them that due to my efforts, the businesses in Novardok were closed on Friday afternoon in deference to the Shabbos preparations."

In order to really savor and enjoy the Friday night Shabbos meal, try to limit yourself to small snacks as Shabbos approaches.

If time allows, read the Torah Portion which will be read in the synagogue Shabbos morning. Choose a commentary on the Torah that you feel comfortable learning from (see *Opportunities For Study*, page 153 for suggestions). In addition to advancing your knowledge, you will feel in touch with Jews throughout the world who are studying the same passages. Such learning is invaluable for your own spiritual growth and will enhance the conversation at your Shabbos table. One of the benefits of Shabbos is that it affords us the opportunity to learn Torah, and to share that learning with others.

If you find it difficult to prepare your home for Shabbos, an easy and terrific first step is to buy flowers. Flowers are an excellent way to welcome Shabbos and are an element of observance that everyone can appreciate and enjoy.

Shabbos Bread—Challah

You can buy challah for Shabbos, but many people, if they have the time, prefer to bake their own. (A suggested recipe is provided in *Shabbos Recipes*, pages 160-161.) The Kabbalists teach that by baking the challah you can invest the bread of Shabbos with a special holiness. "Between the braids" you can infuse your hopes and dreams. Such is the exalted food befitting the Shabbos table.

If you do find the time to bake bread, there is a special mitzvah to remove a small piece of dough called "challah." When you buy bread, part of the kosher supervision is that this piece of "challah" has already been taken off. But if you are making your own, keep the following in mind:

The Torah (Numbers 15:20) tells us, "The first of your dough shall be taken as a tithe." Torah commentators explain that this portion was given to the priests (or in Hebrew, *Kohanim*)[2] to support them in their spiritual endeavors. The point of this mitzvah is that even as we are involved in our physical sustenance we should not forget the spiritual mission of our people.

Additionally, the commentators explain that when this mitzvah is done with the bread, the bread itself becomes elevated. As such it is both food for the body as well as food for the soul.[3]

Taking Challah

This procedure is called "taking challah." Here's how to do it. When your dough is ready to be formed into loaves, put all the dough together in one bowl. Then remove a small (olive size) piece of dough as you say "Behold this is challah." If the recipe includes five pounds of flour or more, you recite the following blessing *before* taking challah:

Baruch Atah Ado-noy Elo-heinu Melech haolam asher kidishanu bimitzvosov vitziyvanu lihafrish challah.

(Blessed are You G-d, King of the universe,
Who sanctified us with His commandments,
and commanded us to separate challah.)

Today, because the priests are not considered ritually pure, they cannot eat this portion which is invested with special holiness. Instead, the bread should be burned. One method is to flatten the dough on a piece of aluminum foil, and place it on the bottom of the oven. Leave it there until it is totally burned. Others save the pieces and burn them before Passover with other bread products. In any case, keep the piece of challah separate and make sure that it does not touch the other loaves while they are baking.

You will find that the word "challah" is commonly used to refer to the Shabbos breads themselves. This usage developed as a result of people's love for this mitzvah and their desire for a reminder that challah be taken. They therefore called bread by the name "challah," to remind them of the mitzvah that is associated with bread.[4]

Setting the Table

♦ Kiddush cup and wine or grape juice.
♦ Challah board, challah cover, a knife and two challohs.

♦ Salt.

♦ Set the table as you would for any special occasion—silverware, fine china, cups, drinks and so on.

♦ Flowers add color and set the tone for a wonderful Shabbos meal.

Candle-lighting

Every Friday evening, as the sun begins to set, Jewish women around the world pave the way for accepting Shabbos. As the time of Shabbos approaches, Jewish women initiate the acceptance of Shabbos, eighteen minutes before actual sundown. They light the Shabbos candles, and the glowing warmth of Shabbos envelops the Jewish home.

The purpose of the Shabbos candles is to add light and joy to the Jewish home. It is a mitzvah that applies equally to men and women. Thus single men, and men whose wives are away, should light candles for the home. Nevertheless, women are given first rights to perform this mitzvah. As the following story illustrates it is a mitzvah of great meaning.

Amy is a social worker who lives in a suburb of Chicago. Although not observant, she enjoys spending an occasional Shabbos in the nearby observant community. The warmth and harmony make her feel good, and she feels at home.

One of her favorite moments is the onset of Shabbos, when she lights her own Shabbos candles. "Lighting Shabbos candles brings light into the world," her Rabbi had said.

But the most meaningful explanation comes from her hostess, Rachel, who often invites Amy to her home for Shabbos. Rachel has the custom of adding one candle for each of her children. "The extra candles symbolize that each child brings his or her unique light into the world. Each child's potential, even their very presence, makes the world a brighter place for everyone."

The Shabbos candles on Friday night are not the only candles that a Jewish woman gets to light. Our Rabbis teach that "the candle of G-d is the soul of a person."[5] It is the woman who has the privilege of bringing children into the world and raising them, so that their "candles" may grow into strong and healthy, light-giving flames.

Candle-lighting is therefore an opportune time for mothers to pray for success in raising their children. The following is an excerpt of the accepted prayer:

May it be Your will, G-d, that You grace me and my husband to raise children who are wise and understanding and light up the world with Torah and good deeds. Please hear my supplication in the merit of our Mothers, Sarah, Rebecca, Rachel and Leah.

Our Matriarchs play a special role in the mitzvah of lighting candles. As we light the candles, we connect with their legacy. The realization that our life challenges are much like theirs, makes the Shabbos candles even more meaningful. Just as they founded families committed to morality and goodness, so do we. Just as their lights were eternal, so we hope that our lights will symbolize the eternal legacy of the Jewish people.

So, as you light the Shabbos candles, imagine your ancestors doing the same. Experience the serenity that Shabbos brings. Recognize that it is the light of Shabbos that has kept the Jew alive throughout the ages, and it is the light of Shabbos that will ensure the stability of the Jewish home.[6]

Candle-lighting is often the mitzvah that brings the light of Shabbos into people's homes. It is a wonderful turning point in the search for spirituality, as this story illustrates.

Linda Greenwald, or Leah, as she now likes to be called, is an eight-year-old student in a small New Jersey day school. Her parents rejected the local public school in the hope that Linda would get a proper Jewish education. Their investment paid off, as she developed a strong sense of Jewish pride and identity. Unfortunately, Shabbos in their home has been non-existent. That is, until last Shabbos.

Linda came home from school ecstatic about what she had learned about lighting the Shabbos candles. The laws and customs of Judaism had made a deep impression on her; now, here was a law that she could grasp onto and identify with. And so it was just minutes before Shabbos that Linda lit the Shabbos candles. Her parents watched with surprise, and realized how meaningful the candles were to their daughter. Deeply moved, they resolved to learn more about their heritage. The radiance of Shabbos had been lost for two generations, but Shabbos will yet be joyfully revived in the Greenwald home.

Candle-lighting
♦ ♦ ♦ *How to do it* ♦ ♦ ♦

1. Choose a place near the Shabbos table where the candles will be secure. A sturdy table out of the reach of young children will do just fine. For safety reasons, make sure that the candles are away from curtains and are not exposed to an open window. Place a large metal tray beneath the candles for added safety.

2. Purchase the candles that you will light. Traditional Shabbos candles are sold in various quantities. Most common is the large box of seventy-two. The candles should last at least three hours, so that you will enjoy their glow well into the meal. Another type of candle on the market, with a graceful simplicity about it, is sold in little glass containers. The candle burns nicely and changes to liquid as it burns. The one drawback is that the glass containers have to be cleaned regularly to maintain the beauty of the glow.

3. Prepare the matches and arrange the candles. Married women, can involve their husbands by having them arrange the candles. Make sure that everything is ready in plenty of time, so you won't be rushed when the time comes to light the candles.

The Candle-lighting Blessing

Finally, at candle-lighting time (eighteen minutes before sunset) light the candles. After lighting the candles, cover your eyes with your hands and recite the blessing:

Baruch Atah Ado-noy Elo-heinu Melech haolam, asher kidishanu bimitzvosov vitziyvanu lihadlik ner shel Shabbos.

(Blessed are You, G-d, King of the universe
Who sanctified us with His commandments
and commanded us to kindle the light of Shabbos.)

When you open your eyes, take a good look at the candles and experience the serenity of the moment, as the eternal glow of Shabbos enters your heart and home.

♦ ♦ ♦ *Candle-Lighting Quick Facts* ♦ ♦ ♦

♦ The time to light the Shabbos candles is slightly before sunset. The prevalent custom, here in the United States, is to do so eighteen minutes before sunset. (In Jerusalem, the custom is to light candles 30-40 minutes before sunset.) The number eighteen has positive connotations,[7] but as a practical matter it shows our eagerness to accept Shabbos early and it ensures that the candles will be lit properly before sunset.

♦ The mitzvah of candle-lighting is done with two candles. One candle corresponds to the positive commandments of Shabbos, and the other to the prohibitions. Alternately, the two candles represent the light that a husband and wife hope to radiate in their Jewish home. Some people light an extra candle for each child they have.

♦ Although candle-lighting is considered the woman's mitzvah, men are equally obligated in the lighting.[8] Therefore, single men, or men whose wives are away, should light candles for the home.

♦ There is a custom to wave your hands towards yourself after lighting the candles, before making the blessing. By waving our hands from the candles to ourselves, we symbolize our readiness to accept the radiance of Shabbos into our lives.

♦ It is proper to cover your eyes before reciting the blessing. Only after the blessing is recited, and the Shabbos has begun, do we open our eyes, and enjoy the light of the candles.[8a]

♦ Even when many married women are together in the same home, they each light Shabbos candles.[9] This is because the

Shabbos lights are meant to create happiness in the home. It follows that the more lights there are, the more happiness is generated.

♦ Many women with children take advantage of the serenity of the moment, and pray for Divine assistance in the raising of their children. Actually, this is an ideal time for meaningful prayer of any kind.

The Source of Blessing

he Friday evening service, during which we welcome the Shabbos Queen, contains numerous paragraphs taken from the Psalms of King David. These Psalms (notably Psalms 95-99) discuss our eternal relationship with G-d.

A high point of the Friday evening service is when we sing the *Lecho Dodi*, a song composed by Rabbi Shlomo Alkabetz (1505-1584, Israel) of the Jewish community in Safed. A noted Kabbalist, he dedicated this song to the love relationship between Shabbos and the Jewish people. The refrain is, "Go, my beloved, towards the Shabbos Queen, to greet her, and to accept her."

Today the song is a classic, accepted universally throughout the Jewish world. The song is usually sung in unison. It explores the beautiful nature of Shabbos and the blessings it has to offer. The second stanza is particularly insightful. It begins:

"Towards the Shabbos, let us arise and go."

We readily acknowledge that the laws of Shabbos can be difficult. Accepting the laws of Shabbos may mean changes of lifestyle and a need to alter old habits. Some favorite activities may have to be canceled or postponed.

Nevertheless, "Let us arise." Let us gather ourselves together and meet the challenge of keeping Shabbos.

"For it is the source of blessing."

Tradition teaches that Shabbos brings with it many forms of blessing. One of the more obvious benefits is the serenity of Shabbos, which gives us the opportunity to assess our direction in life and to strengthen our relationship with our loved ones. At life's close, few people will lament, "I should have worked harder in my business." Many people, however, will wish that they had spent more time with the people they love, as the following stories illustrate.

Shmuel Lipkin is the popular, charismatic Rabbi of a prestigious synagogue in Los Angles, California. His Wednesday night Bible class is always well attended. Week after week his listeners are enthralled by his casual style and his innovative insights. This particular Wednesday night was no different.

Rabbi Lipkin began the class with a smile, saying that he had a serious question to ask the group. After getting everyone's attention, he asked, "What is it that you would be willing to give your life for?"

The question took his audience by surprise, but the answers weren't long in coming.

"I would be willing to die if it was a choice between me and my children," one woman offered.

"I would be willing to give up my life so as not to convert," another stated.

"I would be willing to die rather than be taken prisoner," an army reservist responded.

Finally, the Rabbi raised his hand and said, "Let me clarify something, please. No one is asking you to *die* for the things that you hold dear. I am simply suggesting that you should take the time to *live* for them. Enjoy your freedom, your family, and your children. Take time to go on vacation, to relax, to enjoy life, and to learn about your religion. No one is asking you to die for these ideals. Rather, let's discuss how you can *live* for them."

Additionally, Shabbos gives us quality time with the people we care about—and our relationships with family and friends grow stronger.

Another example of this important lesson is Harvey Gold, a highly successful real estate broker in Denver, Colorado. Over the years his accounts have grown, and today his firm is one of the largest in the region. For a long while Harvey would leave his home early in the morning and arrive back late at night. Slowly, he came to realize that such a schedule was unacceptable.

Recently, Mr. Gold committed himself to becoming a Shabbos observer. When asked about his decision, he explains, "I recognized that my continually expanding business was leaving me little time for myself or my family. By committing myself to keeping Shabbos, I am ensuring that my own sanity and value system do not suffer."

Through keeping the laws of Shabbos we create a higher purpose in our lives. Our accomplishments take on new meaning, as our lives are infused with a special flavor. A Shabbos observer may well admit that it is difficult to keep all its laws. But it is equally true that Shabbos pays rich dividends in quality time spent with one's family. Investing in Shabbos is a worthwhile investment.

Sometimes we worry about business opportunities that we may lose as a result of Shabbos observance. The following parable is most insightful.

A man went to his Rabbi complaining that his business was failing, and he didn't know what to do. The Rabbi asked him, "Do you close your store on Shabbos?"

The man admitted that he did not, whereupon the Rabbi said, "If the Shabbos—which is the source of blessing—is not happy with you, then what can I possibly do?"

The man fell silent as the Rabbi continued, "I'll make a deal with you. If you grant me a fifteen percent share in the profits of your business, I will guarantee that you will succeed."

Seeing the gentleman's willingness, the Rabbi concluded with a twinkle in his eye, "...But I don't want the fifteen percent for myself. I want you to give it entirely to Shabbos. One day out of seven, I want you to close your store. Then, if Shabbos is happy with you, you will be guaranteed success."[10]

Our relationship with Shabbos is a very real one. We go out of our way to honor Shabbos, and in return Shabbos infuses us with strength and success. Although Shabbos can not make a businessman out of one who is not, Shabbos can offer the necessary spark to make things work.

We are told: The Shabbos complained that she had no mate. The six days of the week could each pair up as mates, but the seventh day was the "odd person out." G-d responded, and said, "You, too, shall find a mate...the Jewish people."[11]

Shabbos is our partner, not only in business, but in our entire life. Together with the Shabbos, we attest to the fact that

G-d created the world in six days, and on the seventh day He rested. Just as G-d rested from His creation on the day of Shabbos, so we too refrain from certain actions on the day of Shabbos. As with any relationship, the more effort that we put into it, the more we will gain.

One of the obstacles that prevents many Jews from observing Shabbos is that they feel that if they can't keep all the laws it isn't worth keeping any. This represents a misunderstanding as to how G-d calculates a person's accomplishments. In Jewish thought, there is no concept that someone is all evil or completely perfect. G-d is more sophisticated than that. When G-d makes the accounting, everything is taken into account. Our job is to "grab" as many mitzvohs (good deeds) as we can, and not to get discouraged even if there are some mitzvohs that we cannot yet do.[12]

The Talmud asks: Why is it that Nevuchadnetzar (who destroyed the first Temple in Jerusalem) merited three generations of monarchy? Because in his youth, he worked as a scribe in the king's palace. One day a letter was sent to the king of the Jews, and it did not properly salute the G-d of Israel. Nevuchadnetzar was momentarily troubled by the slight of honor to G-d, and he took three steps in an effort to retrieve the letter. In the merit of those three steps, he was granted three generations of monarchy.[13]

If such is the reward given to an evil person, how much more reward can we expect for each good deed.

I recently encountered a couple who own a large retail store that they "can't close on Shabbos." Although they send their son to a yeshiva day school, Shabbos in their home cannot be found. They feel that since they can't both observe the entire Shabbos, they can't observe *any* of its mitzvohs.

I suggested that they give their child a real Shabbos meal on Friday evening. On Shabbos morning, let one parent stay home, so that the child can attend synagogue and experience the Shabbos service. Enjoy the Shabbos; let it grow on you. Partial observance is certainly better than none at all.[14]

Interestingly, among Jewish observances, it is Shabbos that is considered the sign of the Jew. The Chofetz Chaim (1839-1933, Polish Lithuania) explained that Shabbos observance is like the sign on a storefront. As long as the sign is up, the business is active. Even if the business is floundering, it is still considered open. Once the sign goes down, it doesn't matter how much merchandise exists. If the sign is down, then the store is closed.[15]

Similarly, Shabbos is the store front sign of the Jew. A home that knows the pleasantness of Shabbos has declared itself an active part of the Jewish people, committed to its perpetuation and to its continuity.

Let's return to the next verse in *Lecho Dodi*.

"From the beginning it was crowned. It was the last creation, but it was the original intent."

Just as in life one may go to great lengths to build something, and it is the final efforts that justify all that preceded it, similarly, the Shabbos was created last, but it is the very purpose of creation. The entire world was waiting for the wonderful

Shabbos Queen, and when she came, creation was complete. And so we conclude:

"Let us go, my friend, towards the Shabbos Queen, To greet her, and to accept her."

We prepare to accept on ourselves the responsibilities of Shabbos, but we also prepare to accept the goodness and blessing that Shabbos brings with her. We realize that Shabbos is a gift that G-d gave us to enjoy and to appreciate. Through it we are able to rise spiritually and come closer to our Jewish heritage. Let us bear in mind that Shabbos takes a lifetime of investment, but it is also the investment of a lifetime.

Friday Night

Our Sages tell us that on Friday night, two angels accompany the Jew from the synagogue to witness the holiness of each Jewish home. The angels will view the Shabbos food, the harmony and serenity. They are well aware of the sacrifices you made to arrive at this moment. They say, "Blessed is this Jewish home. May they continue to celebrate many Shabbosos in health and happiness."[16]

In turn, we welcome the angels with the first song of the evening, *Shalom Aleichem*. We sing "Peace unto you, angels of the King of kings." Our focus is not really on the angels but rather on G-d whom they represent. Ultimately, our Shabbos preparations were done to welcome G-d into our homes. Keep in mind the wonderful words of Rabbi Menachem Mendel of Kotzk: (1787-1859, Poland): "Where can G-d be found? Wherever man lets Him in!"

We are now ready to sing *Eishes Chayil*,[17] which praises the woman of the home. Tradition tells us that the heart of the Jewish home is the Jewish wife and mother. She is the stabilizing force in Jewish life. "Far from pearls is her worth," (Proverbs 31:10) is one of the verses of this meaningful song. We do not say that her value is *more* than pearls, but rather *far* from pearls. The two cannot even be compared—the Jewish wife and mother represents life itself.

Blessing the Children

Friday night is the customary time to bless one's children. The blessing for boys refers to Joseph's two sons, Efraim and Menashe. Although Joseph's sons were raised in Egypt, they maintained their allegiance to the faith of Israel. Similarly, we pray that our sons see beyond the tests of peer pressure and the secular world, and maintain lives of righteousness and morality.

The blessing for girls makes reference to the Matriarchs of our people. Just as the Matriarchs founded eternally blessed homes so may our daughters be blessed to build stable Jewish homes.

Place your hands on your child's head and say:

For boys:
Yisimcha Elo-him kiEfrayim vichiMenashe.
(May G-d make you like Efraim and Menashe.)

For girls:
Yisiymeich Elo-him kiSoroh Rivkah Rochel viLeah.
(May G-d make you like Sarah, Rebecca, Rachel and Leah.)

Continue here for each child:
Yivorechicha Ado-noy viyishmirecho.
Yoer Ado-noy ponov elechah viychunekoh.
Yisoh Ado-noy ponov elechah viyoseim lichah shalom.
(May G-d bless you and guard you. May G-d shine His countenance upon you and grace you. May G-d bring His presence to you and grant you the blessing of peace.)

Kiddush

Kiddush is a prayer said over wine or grape juice. The prayer of Kiddush describes the sanctity of the Shabbos and the holiness of the Jewish people. Jewish law teaches that kiddush is inextricably bound to the Shabbos meal. Thus we are told, "The mitzvah of kiddush can only be fulfilled in the same place as the Shabbos meal."[18] This leads to an interesting custom practiced on Friday night in many synagogues.

In many synagogues, at the conclusion of the Friday night service, the Cantor (also called the Chazan) recites the kiddush for the congregation. But instead of drinking the wine or grape juice (as is normally done after someone makes kiddush) the Cantor distributes the grape juice to the children who are present. If the Cantor recites the kiddush, shouldn't he be the one to drink the wine or grape juice?

This custom dates back many generations. During the time when it began, it was unfortunately common that many Jews were homeless. These people would sleep on the synagogue premises, and eat whatever food they happened to have. To ensure that these people would properly fulfill the mitzvah of kiddush, the Rabbis instituted the synagogue kiddush.[19]

In our time, thank G-d, most Jews have homes of their own and can make kiddush for themselves. Nevertheless, this custom has been with us for so many years that we are hesitant to abolish it (as explained below). The problem is that the kiddush has to be recited for somebody. The kiddush is not for the Cantor, because kiddush can only be made where the Shabbos meal will be eaten, and the Cantor intends to eat at his home.

In order for this custom to continue, an interesting solution was instituted. The Cantor recites the kiddush, and then distributes the wine or grape juice to the young children. These children should be young enough that they are not required to wait for "the real" kiddush, but old enough to understand that there is a mitzvah of kiddush. In this way, the kiddush can be said in the synagogue and because the children are drinking, its recital is not in vain.[20]

The concept that we are hesitant to abolish old customs requires clarification. Does this mean that we will continue a custom even when it is no longer applicable?

The importance of Jewish customs can be understood in light of the Talmud's praise of the Jewish people. "Even if they are not prophets, they are children of prophets."[21] There are good reasons for every custom. Our sages were hesitant to abolish an established custom, even when they could find no explanation for it. Invariably after research a reason is discovered.

Additionally, Jewish life has a tendency to repeat itself. In our time, although most people have homes, some will not be eating a Shabbos meal at home. Often, single members of a family express an interest in Jewish practice, but will not necessarily have a Shabbos meal at home. It is most proper that their friends extend a Shabbos invitation to them. If however, this isn't feasible, it is possible to fulfill the mitzvah of kiddush with the synagogue kiddush. They should eat (at least some cake) following the kiddush, and they will be fulfilling the mitzvah in accordance with the rule that, "The mitzvah of kiddush can only be fulfilled in the same place as the Shabbos meal."[22]

Kiddush
♦ ♦ ♦ *How to do it* ♦ ♦ ♦

Kiddush is said while holding a cup of wine or grape juice. It is customary to use a beautiful cup or silver goblet which holds at least four and a half ounces of liquid.[23]

Friday night Kiddush consists of three parts. In the first paragraph, we testify that G-d created the world and rested on the seventh day. We affirm our belief in G-d, that G-d created the world, and that He did so for a purpose. Through this affirmation our lives take on a sense of higher meaning.

Next we say the blessing on the wine. This blessing is not specific to Shabbos. Before eating or drinking anything, we make a blessing to acknowledge our thankfulness to G-d.[24] Because we will drink the wine at the conclusion of the kiddush, this blessing is incorporated in the kiddush.

In the final part of kiddush we affirm the sanctity of Shabbos and of the Jewish people who observe it. Tradition tells us that G-d offered the Torah to all the nations of the world, and they all refused it because of the higher calling which it required. It was only the Jews who gladly answered G-d's question with an exclamation of acceptance (see Exodus 24:7). This ancient acceptance created the bond between the Torah and the Jewish people that still exists in our time.

If you have the opportunity to spend Shabbos with different families, you may find that some people stand for the entire kiddush, while others sit. Still others begin saying the kiddush while standing, and then sit down for the second two sections. While the first two customs are readily understandable (either we sit or we stand) the third custom requires explanation.

This custom can be explained based on the fact that the first part of kiddush is a testimony, where we state our belief in the Creator. As such, it is said while standing, just as all testimony (in a Jewish court of law) is said while standing.[25] The remaining two parts of kiddush are the essence of kiddush. As such, they are said while sitting, in accordance with the rule that "Kiddush should be said in the place of the meal." Since we sit down when we are ready to begin a meal, sitting is appropriate for the second part of kiddush.

After the kiddush is recited, the wine is distributed to everyone. You are not obligated to drink from the kiddush wine, nevertheless it is proper to do so.[26] There is no need for you to recite a blessing over the wine since that was already included in the recital of kiddush. If, however, you talked before drinking the wine, then a new blessing (*Hagofen*) should be recited but the entire kiddush need not be repeated.[27]

♦ ♦ ♦ *Kiddush* ♦ ♦ ♦
Transliteration & Translation

in an undertone:
Vayihiy erev, vayihiy boker

continue aloud:
Yom hashishi
Vayichulu hashomayim vihoaretz vichol tzivoam.
Vayichal Elo-him bayom hashiviyie milachto asher asa,

vayishbos bayom hashiviyie mikol milachto asher asa.
Vayivorech Elo-him es yom hashiviyie vayikadeish oso,
key vo shovas mikol milachto asher boro Elo-him laasos.

(And it was evening, then morning of the sixth day.
And creation of heaven and earth were completed with
all of their forces. On the seventh day G-d completed
all of creation, and He rested on the seventh day
from all that He had done. G-d blessed the seventh day
and sanctified it, for on it G-d rested from all of creation
that He had done. Genesis 2:1-3.)

Then recite the blessing over the wine or grape juice:

Baruch Atah Ado-noy Elo-heinu Melech haolam
borei piri hagofen.

(Blessed are You G-d, King of the universe
Who created the fruit of the vine.)

This is the final part of kiddush:

Baruch Atah Ado-noy Elo-heinu Melech haolam,
asher kidishanu bimitzvosov virotzoh vonu,
viShabbos kodsho biahavoh uvirotzon hinchilanu
zikoron limaaseh bireishis. Key hu yom tichilah
limikroey kodesh zeicher litziyas mitzroyim.
Key vonu vocharto viosonu kidashtoh mikol hoamim,
viShabbos kodshichoh biahavoh uvirotzon hinchaltonu.
Baruch Atah Ado-noy mikadeish haShabbos.

(Blessed are You G-d, King of the universe, Who sanctified
us with His commandments as He desired us, and gave us in

love and pleasure the day of Shabbos as an inheritance, to remember the act of creation. For Shabbos is the first of the holidays which are a reminder of the Exodus from Egypt. For G-d chose us and sanctified us from amongst the nations, and with love and pleasure He gave us the holy Shabbos. Blessed are You G-d Who sanctifies the Shabbos.)

♦ ♦ ♦ *Quick Facts About Kiddush* ♦ ♦ ♦

♦ Kiddush means sanctification. The words of kiddush discuss the love relationship between G-d and the Jewish people, and the gift of Shabbos that G-d gave us.

♦ It is customary for the male head of the household to recite the kiddush, although women are equally included in this mitzvah.

♦ You can fulfill this mitzvah by listening to another person's recital, provided that you pay attention and that that person intends to include you. Therefore, if you are a guest at someone's house, it is best to clarify whether you will be making your own kiddush or if you wish to be included in the kiddush of your host.[28]

♦ Kiddush is recited twice on Shabbos, once on Friday night and then again on the following day after the morning services. Although the texts are different, they both contain the basic blessing made over wine. The Friday night kiddush emphasizes G-d's act of creation, which was completed on Shabbos. The Shabbos day kiddush tells of G-d's covenant with Israel and the sanctity with which we experience the Shabbos.

♦ During kiddush, the challah should be covered. A fancy

challah cover (that can be purchased in any Judaica store) is great, but a simple napkin is sufficient. We cover the bread for an interesting reason. We want to ensure that the challah is not insulted that we make kiddush over the wine and ignore the challah. Commentators point out that the issue here is not the shame of the challah. After all, bread is inanimate, and clearly doesn't care one way or the other. The true lesson here is not for the challah, but for us. Shabbos represents unity and harmony; our intent is to be peaceful. Such sublime goals are possible only when we are sensitive to the feelings of others.[29]

Hand-washing

Before eating bread we wash our hands in a ritual manner. The concept of hand-washing has its roots in the purity present in the time of the holy Temple in Jerusalem.[30] (The second Temple stood from c. 350 BCE until the year 70 CE when it was destroyed by the Romans.) Ritual washing of our hands before eating bread is one of the few vestiges of that glorious period when it was common for Jews to maintain a higher level of purity and cleanliness. It is with hope and prayer that we yearn for the day that the Temple will be rebuilt.

Hand-washing
♦ ♦ ♦ *How to do it* ♦ ♦ ♦

Take a cup that holds at least four and a half ounces.[31] Special washing cups with two handles are sold in Jewish neighborhoods and are particularly useful for this purpose.

Second, check to make sure that your hands are clean so

that the water will spread evenly across your hand. Rings should be removed until after you dry your hands.

Now you are ready to wash. Fill the cup with water and hold it in your left hand. Pour the water smoothly over your right hand until your wrist. Then pour a second time on the same hand. Switch the cup to the right hand and repeat the same two pourings on the left hand. If you run out of water simply refill the cup and keep on going.[32]

Before drying your hands, recite the blessing:

"Baruch Atah Ado-noy Elo-heinu Melech haolam, asher kidishanu bimitzvosov vitziyvanu al nitilas yodoyim."

(Blessed are You, G-d, King of the universe Who
sanctified us with His commandments
and commanded us regarding washing the hands.)

*Remember, no talking until after the blessing
on the bread is made and you have eaten from it.*

Blessing on the Bread

After hand-washing we return to the table and begin the meal. The head of the household lifts the two challah loaves and says the blessing over bread.

**Baruch Atah Ado-noy Elo-heinu Melech haolam,
hamotzi lechem min haoretz.**

(Blessed are You, G-d, King of the universe
Who brings forth bread from the earth.)

We use two challah loaves for a particular reason. In the

desert, after the Exodus from Egypt, the manna did not fall on Shabbos. Instead, a double portion fell on Friday (see Exodus 16: 4-30). By using two loaves at our Shabbos meal, we remind ourselves of the sanctity of Shabbos and that G-d will provide for our material needs. The double portion that fell for our ancestors in the desert is the symbol that the Shabbos observer will not lose out because of his observance.

One of the loaves is cut and the bread is distributed to everyone. It is customary to dip the slices into some salt just as the sacrifices in the Temple were salted before being consumed (see Leviticus 2:13). We are aware that the potentially elevated status of the Shabbos table is tremendous, so we are wont to imitate the laws of the Temple.

The Shabbos Meal

There is a mitzvah to have a special Shabbos meal. Traditionally, the meal includes some kind of fish,[33] soup and chicken or meat. If you dislike meat or poultry you can adjust the menu accordingly. If you have children, try to prepare some of their favorite dishes. Point out the items that they enjoy. Explain that these foods are in honor of Shabbos, thereby building their excitement for this day.

The Shabbos meal is the perfect time for strengthening family relationships. When considering an increased commitment to Shabbos observance, it is common for family members to express different levels of interest. The goal should always be to experience Shabbos with an excitement that will make it enjoyable for everyone to participate. The Shabbos table is the perfect place to strive for tolerance and unity.[34]

Shabbos Songs

On Shabbos we enjoy plentiful, delicious food and take the time to thank G-d for it. In this joyous frame of mind, it is easier to sing the delightful Shabbos melodies, or *zemiros*. Many of these songs were authored by the sages and Kabbalists of old, and contain exalted insights into the secrets of creation. You can choose from any of the many Shabbos songs that are printed in the prayer book, of which some popular examples appear below. If you visit different families for Shabbos, you will find that every family has their own favorite melodies.

Torah Thoughts

Just as the meal is important for our physical enjoyment, so too we also ensure the fulfillment of our spiritual needs. The discussion of the weekly Torah portion is one method of introducing spirituality into the meal. (See *Opportunities for Study* for suggested books and p. 53 for some ideas to help in preparing a Torah thought.) If there are children present, be sure to include them in the discussions. Often, lessons oriented to children are of such basic importance that everyone can relate to and learn from them.

Some Classic Shabbos Songs

Here are some classic songs that are sung at the Friday night meal. We have included both the transliteration and the translation of each song.

Minucha Visimcha
Rest and Happiness

Minucha visimcha ohr layihudim
Rest and happiness—light to the Jews;
Yom shabboson yom machmadim
It is the day of Shabbos, a day we hold dear.
Shomrov vizochrov heimo miiydim
Those who observe it testify,
Key lishishah kol biruim viomidim.
that in six days all was created [including...]

Shimey shomayim eretz viyamim
The heavens, the land and the sea,
Kol tzivoh morom gevohim viromim
all forces of high, and all the high places,
Tanin viodom vichayas rieymim
the fish, man and the animals;
Key bikoh Hashem tzur olomim.
for G-d is the support for the entire universe.

Hu asher diyber liam sigulaso
About Shabbos G-d spoke to His treasured nation,
Shomor likadisho mibowo viad tzeiso
"Guard its sanctity from its beginning to its end."
Shabbos kodesh yom chemdoso
G-d holds the holy Shabbos dear,
Key voh shovas Keil mikol milachto.
for on it He rested from His creation.

31

Bimitzvahs Shabbos Keil yachalitzoch
Through the mitzvah of Shabbos G-d will redeem you.
Kum kiroh eilov yochish liamitzoch
Arise! call to Him; He will strengthen you.
Nishmas kol chai vigam naaritzoch
(We recite,) "All the living,"
and also, "We proclaim your strength."
Echol bisimchoh key chivor rotzoch.
Eat with joy, for He has favored you.

Bimishneh lechem vikeydush raboh
With double bread and special kiddush;
Birov matamim viruach nidiyvah
with good tasting food and a devoted spirit.
Yizku lirav tuv hamisangim boh
May those who enjoy Shabbos merit all that is good,
Biviyas goel lichayey haolam haboh.
with the coming of the Redeemer and the World to Come.

◆ ◆ ◆

Koh Ribon
G-d, the Master

Chorus: **Koh ribon olam violmayoh Ahnt hu malkoh
Melech malchayoh.**
Master of the universe: You are the King, the King of kings,
**Ovad givurteich visimhayoh shifar kodomoch
lihachavayoh.**
The work of Your might and the miracles,

32

it is proper to declare before You.

Shivochin asader tzafroh viramshoh
I compose praise each morning and night
Loch elokoh kadishoh, di viroh kol nafshoh
To You, O G-d, Who created all life [including]
Iyrin kadishin uvinei enoshoh
The holy angels and man
Cheivas biroh viofey shimayoh.
The animals of the field and the birds of the heavens.

Ravrivin ovdeich visakifin
Great and powerful are Your deeds
Mochich rimayoh vizakeif kififin
You humble the haughty and straighten the bent
Lu yichyeh givar shinin alfin
Even if man would live thousands of years
Lo yeol givurteich bichusbinayoh.
He would be unable to calculate Your greatness.

Elokoh di lei yikar urivusoh
G-d to Whom is honor and greatness
Pirok yas onoch miypum aryivosoh
Redeem Your flock from the mouth of the lions
Viapeik yas ameich migoy golusoh
Take Your nation out of the exile
Ameich di vichart mikol umayoh.
The nation that You have chosen from among the others.

Limikdosheich tuv ulikodesh kudshin

33

Return to Your Sanctuary, to the holy of holies
Asar di vei yechdun ruchin vinafshin
The place that souls and spirits will rejoice
Viyzamrun loch shirin virachshin
And they will sing to You songs and praises
Biyrushleim kartoh dishufrayoh.
In Jerusalem, the city of beauty.

Grace After Meals

When we finish eating, we turn our attention to the Grace after meals. The theme of Grace is that we wish to relate to G-d under all circumstances. Before we ate, even if we were very hungry, we stopped for a moment to concentrate and thank G-d for the food. Now that we are satiated, we again pause to express our appreciation. These two times are representative of the challenges of life. People may forget G-d when they are hungry and the going is rough. Conversely, satiation and leisure may bring about forgetfulness of spirituality. Shabbos serves as a reminder that we can relate to G-d in all circumstances.[35]

Before we begin Grace, some families pass around a cup of water and a bowl, to rinse our hands before these prayers. It's a way of really ending the meal. Pour a few drops of water on your hands and then rub them together.

Interestingly, the general custom is that women do not wash. The simplest explanation is that since they are in and out of the kitchen to serve the meal, it is assumed that they wash there before saying Grace.[36]

Grace After Meals
♦ ♦ ♦ *How to do it* ♦ ♦ ♦

When three or more men eat together, we precede the Grace after meals with a special introduction. (The name of G-d [*Elo-heinu*] is only recited if ten men participate.)

The designated leader says:
Rabbosai nivoreich
(My friends, let us say grace)

The others respond:
Yehi shem Ado-noy mivoroch mayatoh viad olam
(May the name of G-d be blessed, now and forever)

The leader repeats the above response and then says:
Birishus maranan virabbanan virabosai nivoreich [Elo-heinu] sheachalnu mishelow.
(With permission from you, my esteemed friends, let us recite Grace [to G-d from Whom we ate] to Him from Whom we ate.)

The others respond:
Baruch [Elo-heinu] sheachalnu mishelo uvituvow choyinu.
(Blessed is He [G-d] that we ate from His, and through His goodness we live)

The leader repeats this last response:
We then begin Grace as is printed in the prayer book.

Shabbos Morning

Shabbos Morning is the most popular time to attend the synagogue services. If there is a beginner's service, this is definitely the best way to be introduced to the Shabbos service. Or you can try the regular service. Here are some tips to make the experience a pleasure.

A typical Shabbos prayer service runs from about 9:00 to 11:30. The first hour includes the basic prayer service, the next hour and a half contains the weekly Torah reading, the Rabbi's sermon and the final service, which usually includes quite a bit of singing. It is the last hour or hour and a half that the beginner will find most interesting.

In traditional synagogues you will find separate sections for men and women; this is the traditional manner for communal prayer. In many synagogues, a kiddush follows the services. At that time socializing is open and encouraged.

In many large synagogues new people sometimes get lost in the crowd. When I attend a synagogue for the first time, I often ask someone to show me an unoccupied seat. Invariably this request leads to introductions and invitations. Keep in mind that there are times during prayer that it is not proper to speak. So if a congregant uses sign language to guide you to a seat, don't be surprised. He or she is simply at a point in the prayers when it is not proper to speak.

Even veteran congregants may feel awkward when meeting

new people. A simple nod and smile can do wonders to make everyone comfortable.

The prayers in traditional congregations are almost entirely in Hebrew. Fortunately there are a number of good English translations, as well as transliterations for the singing parts. Alternatively, you may wish to peruse a book (such as this one) while you wait for a part of the service that you are familiar with.

Although the synagogue's traditional function is communal prayer, the synagogue has become a center for all kinds of community functions. As a social center and an educational facility for interested adults, the synagogue has become central to Jewish life. The greatest gift you can give yourself is the gift of being comfortable in the synagogue.

Wearing the Talis (Prayer Shawl)

It is common for married men to wear a talis, or prayer shawl throughout the morning prayer service. Single men who are honored in the synagogue should also wear a talis. They can either use one of the synagogue's or borrow one from a friend. To put the talis on, find the seam or design on one of the edges of the talis and hold that side up facing you. Then twirl the talis onto your back so that the design is now at your neck facing outward. It may take a few tries to perfect the technique, but as they say, "It's all in the wrist."

Once you are wearing the talis on your back, simply lift and fold the sides so that they rest neatly on your shoulders.

The Honors in the Synagogue

In traditional synagogues, men are given the officiating parts of the prayer service. For example, women are not called to the Torah. This is because the Torah views Judaism as a division of responsibilities. There are some mitzvohs primarily given to women, and others given to men. The Torah assigns to men the mitzvah of communal prayer and the officiation that accompanies it. This should not detract from womens' participation in the main function of the synagogue: *prayer*. Our sages place great importance on the prayers of women. In fact, many laws of prayer are inferred from the prayers of the righteous woman Chanah (see Samuel 1, 1:13 and Talmud Brachos 31a).

Men who attend the synagogue may wish to have a bit of introduction to the possible honors, so I will include a brief overview at this point.

If you enter the synagogue during the Torah reading you will notice that the center of the synagogue is the center of attention. It is here where the Torah scroll lies on the bimah, or table. The key people at the bimah are the two people standing in the center facing forward. On the left is the Torah reader, on the right is the congregant honored to make the blessings on that Torah portion. Each Shabbos eight men are chosen for this honor.

The Gabbai or caretaker is the man who assigns the honors. If he decides to call you to the Torah, he will ask for your Hebrew name as well as your father's Hebrew name. When you are called up, simply go to the bimah where you will be shown the place in the Torah. You will recite a blessing before the Torah portion is read and then a second blessing after the reading. If you are uncomfortable reading Hebrew, you can ask for a transliterated copy of the blessings. (See *How to do it* below.)

Another common honor for congregants is to be chosen to open the ark before and after the Torah reading. Each synagogue has its own style for constructing the ark. Generally, there is a rope on the ark's right side to open the curtain. The doors can then be opened either by pulling sideways or out, as the case may be. When the Cantor signals to you, remove the scroll from the ark and give it to the Cantor (often there is more than one scroll, so ask which one to remove). You will then close the ark and remain in place until the Cantor begins the procession to the reading table. Keep in mind that the Torah scroll is held so that it leans against the right shoulder.

As you return to your seat after the honor people will congratulate you on a job well done. A common greeting is "*Yiyasher Kochacho*," which basically means "more power to you." It's like a congratulations and so the polite answer is "Thank You."

Blessings on the Torah
♦ ♦ ♦ *How to do it* ♦ ♦ ♦

Each Shabbos, eight men are called to the Torah. Each man recites a blessing prior to the Torah reading, and then another blessing after the reading.

If you are called up, the procedure is as follows.
The reader will show you the place. Touch the Torah in the margin with a corner of the talis and then kiss the talis. We do this

because we do not touch the Torah directly with our hands.

You will then say:
Borichu es Ado-noy hamivoroch
(Let us bless G-d, the blessed One.)

To which the congregation will respond:
Boruch Ado-noy hamivoroch liolam voed
(May G-d be blessed forever and ever.)

Repeat the congregation's response, then say:
Baruch Atah Ado-noy Elo-heinu Melech haolam,
asher bochar bonu mikol hoamim vinosan lonu es
Torahso. Boruch Atah Ado-noy nosein haTorah.

(Blessed are You G-d, King of the universe,
Who chose us from the nations and gave us the Torah.
Blessed are You G-d the Giver of the Torah.)

The reader then reads the designated portion. Try to follow along
with him.[37] *When he concludes, recite the following blessing:*
Baruch Atah Ado-noy Elo-heinu Melech haolam,
asher nosan lonu Toras emes vichayey olam nota
bisocheinu. Boruch Atah Ado-noy nosein haTorah.

(Blessed are You G-d, King of the universe,
Who gave us the Torah of truth and imbued us with everlasting life. Blessed are You G-d the Giver of the Torah.)

Note: When practicing these blessings, the name of G-d
should not be pronounced (i.e., Ado-noy or Elo-heinu).

♦ ♦ ♦ *The Synagogue Vocabulary* ♦ ♦ ♦

Aliyah—Getting called up to the Torah.

Amen (or Omein)—The traditional response upon hearing a blessing.

Amidah (or Shemoneh Esrei)—The most important selection of the service, recited while standing in silent devotion.

Aron—The ark in which the Torah scrolls are kept. Usually it is the center of attraction in the front of the synagogue.

Chazan—the Cantor.

Chumash—Bible or Pentateuch.

Gabbai—Caretaker, he is in charge of assigning the honors. A good person to talk to if you need assistance.

Gililah—The person who assists during hagbah to roll, wrap and cover the Torah scroll.

Hagbah—Lifting of the Torah. After the reading of the Torah it is customary to lift the Torah.

Hashem—G-d.

Kippah—Contemporary term for the head covering worn by men. Also called yarmulke.

Laining—The reading of the Torah.

Maariv—The evening service.

Minchah—The afternoon service.

Mussaf—The additional Shabbos prayer, recited after the Torah reading and Rabbi's sermon.

Parsha—The Torah portion of the week. Usually the subject of the Rabbi's sermon.

Rav or **Rov**—Rabbi, usually seated in the front facing the congregation.

Shacharis—The morning service.

Shul—A traditional word for synagogue.

Siddur—Prayer book.

Talis—Prayer shawl.

Yarmulke—Traditional term for the head covering worn by men. Also called kippah.

Shabbos Lunch

ollowing the morning services, many synagogues serve kiddush. The kiddush is often hosted by a specific family in honor of some special occasion. It may be in honor of a Bar Mitzvah, Bat Mitzvah, engagement or even a graduation. The appropriate greeting at a kiddush is *"Mazal Tov"* or "Best of Luck." Generally the kiddush will be recited for everyone and after you hear kiddush, you should (make the appropriate blessing—*Mezonos*) and eat cake or cookies to fulfill the obligation of kiddush in the place that you eat. This way, you need not repeat kiddush when you get home. Nevertheless, if when you arrive home you wish to repeat kiddush for those who were not in synagogue, you may do so.

When you return home you will begin the second Shabbos meal. This meal is similar to the Friday night meal. Kiddush is recited (a different text is used at this meal, see adjoining page), then we wash our hands and recite the blessing over bread. The bread is distributed and the meal proceeds according to your preferences. A hot dish should be included. The chulent stew is probably the most common hot food to be served (see pg. 48). As on Friday night, be sure to include songs and Torah thoughts. (See *How to do it*, pg. 53 for some ideas on how to prepare a Torah thought.)

The meal is followed by Grace after meals, after which we

proceed to a restful Shabbos afternoon.

♦ ♦ ♦ *Morning Kiddush* ♦ ♦ ♦
Translation & Transliteration

***Vishomiru binei yisroel es haShabbos,
laasos es haShabbos lidorosom biris olom.
Baynie uveyn binei yisroel os he liolam;
key sheishes yomim oso Ado-noy es hashomayim
vies haaretz, uvayom hashiviyie shovas vayenofash.***

(The Jewish people shall observe the Shabbos, to create the Shabbos for generations as an everlasting covenant. Between Me (G-d) and the Jewish people, it is a sign forever; for in six days G-d created heaven and earth, and on the seventh day He rested and was refreshed. Exodus 31:16-17.)

***Al kein beirach Ado-noy es
yom haShabbos vayikadsheyhu.***

(Therefore G-d blessed and sanctified
the day of Shabbos. Exodus 20:11.)

***Baruch Atah Ado-noy Elo-heinu
Melech haolam, borei piri hagofen.***

(Blessed are You G-d King of the universe,
Who created the fruit of the vine.)

Spiritual Food

As we begin the second Shabbos meal, it is again apparent

that this is a special day. We serve the very best foods and set the table with our finest utensils in honor of Shabbos. The significance of the meal is illustrated by the following story.

The king of a certain country, started a custom in his family. Each year, on the anniversary of his coronation, his family was to celebrate with fanfare.

One year, his son found himself in a small hamlet on the day designated for the festivities. He remembered his father's desire that all his relatives should dance and sing in celebration of the anniversary, but he was surrounded by simple peasants who would not understand the cause for celebration. How could they appreciate his father's benevolence as their ruler and all of his nobility and kindness? After much thought he had an idea.

The prince called together the leaders of this small town, and announced that because of their kindness and goodness, he would treat them to a day of food, wine and music. He invited everyone to the local tavern; the prince would cover the bill.

It didn't take long for the festivities to begin. After all, the prince himself had ordered the people to enjoy themselves. As the drinks and food took effect, the townspeople danced joyously to the accompaniment of the music. Little did they know, they were actually enabling the prince to celebrate the rule of his benevolent father.

Similarly, our souls wish to rejoice and celebrate life and the world that G-d created. But our spiritual souls were placed in physical bodies; in order to rejoice, the soul must make a celebration that the body will appreciate. The Shabbos meal is the means by which the soul can celebrate, and reach the celestial heights for which it yearns.

There is another, perhaps mystical insight, into the unique nature of the Shabbos meal.

The Talmud (Shabbos 119a) tells us that a governor once asked Rabbi Yehoshua ben Chananyah, "Why does your Shabbos food taste so good?"

Rabbi Yehoshua answered, "There is a special spice which we put into the food, and its name is Shabbos."

"So give me some of this wonderful spice."

Rabbi Yehoshua responded, "I cannot give it to you, because it belongs to those who keep Shabbos. By keeping Shabbos we invest the 'Shabbos spice' into the food. One who does not keep the Shabbos cannot obtain this special flavor."

Indeed, many have observed that Shabbos food has a particularly delicious taste. The food itself acquires a special exalted quality as it becomes part of the Shabbos meal. In Judaism, eating is not a simple, mundane endeavor. It is an action which we can invest with holiness, if our intentions are oriented towards spirituality.

Many people view the world as having only two dimensions—physical or spiritual. The truth is that there is another, more sophisticated dimension. It is the physical object or action elevated by humans so that it has become spiritual. "Sanctify G-d's name with that which is permitted."[38] Because we are both physical and spiritual, we have the capability of blending the two to create a new and exalted dimension.

This approach to life manifests itself most clearly on Shabbos. On Shabbos we view all our actions through the special Shabbos lens. All our physical actions take on a spiritual nature. We may eat during the week, but on Shabbos we have a Shabbos meal. During the week we may sleep, but on Shabbos we take a Shabbos nap. It is through such actions that we recognize our goal: To sanctify G-d's name. We come to realize that this can be done simply, in every aspect of our lives.[39]

This is why it is so important to discuss Torah thoughts at the Shabbos meal. Torah thoughts help us focus on Shabbos and the meal itself becomes holy.[40] Similarly, if Shabbos is experienced in holiness, it can sanctify the entire week. Because Shabbos is the soul of the week, through it the mundane becomes sacred. Shabbos gives purpose to life.

Experiencing Shabbos properly requires effort. Even people who have observed Shabbos for many years need constant rejuvenation. Following is a common example.

Marian and Jack are proud Jews who live in a small town in Michigan. Their children are all married and have moved to various towns throughout the country. Marian keeps in contact with them and is proud of their families and accomplishments. But since the children have moved away, she has felt that something was missing from the Shabbos atmosphere.

After considering the matter, she realized that what bothered her most was that the Shabbos meal had lost its vibrancy. They no longer sat together to sing the Shabbos songs. But most of all, Marian missed the excitement of her childrens' Torah discussions.

Marian thought of ways to improve the mood at the Shabbos table. She and Jack make an extra effort to invite guests to share Shabbos with them. But even when they are on their own, Jack always reads aloud from a popular English-Torah text, to the joyful appreciation of his proud and smiling wife.

A Special Shabbos Food
Chulent

The Torah, in Exodus 35:3, tells us, "You shall not burn a fire in your dwelling places on the day of Shabbos." When the Torah was given on Mount Sinai, an oral tradition accompanied it, and stated: This verse prohibits the kindling of a light on Shabbos, but does not prohibit us from leaving a fire burning on its own during Shabbos. Likewise, it is permitted to leave food on the fire during Shabbos until it is needed for the meal.[41]

The Talmud tells us that some Jews (c. 250 BCE-70 CE) did not accept the oral law, and interpreted the Torah literally. They founded a sect called Tzidukim (named after their leader Tzadok, also known as Saduccees) and often acted in a way foreign to Jewish tradition.[42] For example, the Tzidukim prohibited a Jew from leaving a fire burning in his home on the day of Shabbos.[43] To the Rabbis' great chagrin, they would sit in cold and darkness, and eat cold food on Shabbos.

The fact that there is an oral law should be quite obvious from daily life. To illustrate: When a recipe calls for a "dash" of pepper, how do we know how much to put in? How much is a dash? Coupled with all written instructions is a certain amount of tradition and oral guidance. Similarly, in the laws of Shabbos, the oral law guides us with regard to the how, when, where, and why of these laws.

Indeed, it is impossible to interpret the written law without the oral law. For example, with regard to ritual slaughter, the Torah commands us to perform it "as I commanded you" (Deuteronomy 12:21), even though the laws of slaughter are not included in the written law. Clearly, the Torah was referring to the oral law, which outlines the nuances of kosher slaughter. These traditions of the oral law, have become part of the body called *halacha* (or Jewish law) which has guided the Jewish people throughout the ages.

Nevertheless, because of the foolishness of this small group of Jews, the Rabbis decided to take action. In an effort to demonstrate that these Jews were wrong, the Rabbis encouraged the people to have hot food on Shabbos.[46] This would certainly enhance the Shabbos meal, but, more importantly, it would demonstrate our loyalty to the oral law and to Jewish tradition.

Although, technically any hot dish or drink is sufficient, a custom developed in the Northern European and Russian Jewish communities of eating chulent on the day of Shabbos (the *ch* of chulent is pronounced as in charity). The stew—made up of meat, potatoes, barley, beans, and spices—is put up to cook before Shabbos. It remains cooking on a low flame until we are ready to enjoy it for Shabbos lunch. In this way we enjoy hot food at the Shabbos meal, and at the same time, reaffirm our belief in the authenticity of the oral tradition.

In our time, chulent continues to affirm our commitment to Torah law, but it has taken on an additional, unique dimension. For those who are not observant, hot food can be produced any day of the week, Shabbos included. For the observant Jew, however, chulent represents the designated hot food of the Shabbos day. By leaving this stew cooking straight through Shabbos, the observant family is able to enjoy a steamy dish for the Shabbos meal. It is therefore common for chulent to represent an exciting turning point in a person's commitment to Shabbos observance, as the following story illustrates.

Anna is an energetic writer who became observant several years ago. She enjoys the nuances of Jewish living, the holidays, and the newfound meaning in her heritage. There is nothing, however, that she enjoys more than the kind of phone call that she received one Friday.

The call came from a friend who had been grappling with the decision of "becoming observant" for many years. Recently, she added religious observance to her life. She began sending her children to day school, and they celebrated the holidays together as a family. But, somehow, Shabbos observance was a bit more than she was ready for.

That is why Anna was so excited when her friend asked, "How do you make chulent? Could you give me your recipe?" It meant that her friend's hurdle had been overcome. Her friend had decided to add that simple stew to her family's menu. That simple stew, attests to the Jewish people's love for Shabbos, their commitment to keep its laws, and their readiness to reap its benefits.[47]

Judaism, and Shabbos in particular, is a process of continual spiritual growth. The Shabbos table is the ideal place for this important process. Whether it is through the songs, the exchange of ideas, the chulent or the Shabbos chicken, everyone can enjoy Shabbos and identify with it. The family unit grows stronger through the time spent together and the unity that Shabbos fosters.

Here is another classic Shabbos song that can be sung at the Shabbos lunch meal.

Yom Zeh Michubod
This Day is Honored

Chorus:
Yom zeh michubod mikol yomim
key vo shovas tzur olomim.
This day is honored from all the others
for on it G-d rested.

Sheishes yomim taaseh milachtecho
Six days you shall do work,
Viyom hashiviyie leilokecho
the seventh day is dedicated to G-d.
Shabbos lo saaseh vo milocho
On Shabbos do not do work,
Key chol oso sheishes yomim.
for all has been done in six days.

Rishon hu limikroey kodesh
It is the first of the holidays,
Yom shaboson yom Shabbos kodesh
a day of rest, day of Shabbos.
Al kein kol ish biyeyno yikadeish

Therefore we make kiddush on wine,
Al shtei lechem yivtziu simimim.
on two whole loaves we break bread.

Echol mashmanim shisei mamtakim
Eat tasty foods, drink sweet drinks,
Key keil yitein lichol bo diveikim
G-d grants blessing to those who cling to Him:
Beged lilbosh lechem chukim
Clothing to wear, alloted bread
Bosor vidogim vichol matamim.
Meat and fish, and all tasty foods.

Lo sechsar kol bo
You shall be missing nothing,
viochaltoh visovotoh
you will eat and be satisfied
uveirachtoh es Hashem elokeicho asher ohavtoh
and you will bless G-d Whom you love,
Key veirachicho mikol hoamim.
for He has blessed you from among the nations.

Hashomayim misapirim kivodo
The heavens speak of His honor;
Vigam haoretz molah chasdo
the earth is filled with His kindness.
riu key chol eileh osisoh yado
Look! all this is His creation,
key hu hatzur pa'alo somim.
for He is the sustainer, His deeds are complete.

Preparing a Torah Thought
♦ ♦ ♦ *How to do it* ♦ ♦ ♦

The Torah thought (or *dvar Torah*) is an exciting aspect of the Shabbos table. It provides the opportunity to share thoughts about the weekly Torah portion and about Judaism in general.

An inspirational Torah thought can be said in as little as three minutes. But preparation for that short thought can take much longer. Since Shabbos is a learning experience, preparation for the Torah thought is very worthwhile. Here are some ideas on how to go about preparing.

I find it best to start with an Hebrew-English Chumash (Bible) or Siddur (prayer book). If you choose Chumash, preference is given to the Torah portion of that week. The weekly portion is listed on the Hebrew-English calendars available through Jewish organizations or at Judaica stores.

Spend some time learning from the Chumash. Get a feel for the portion that you wish to speak about. After examining the commentary, you may wish to do a bit of research to expand your thoughts in the direction of any major Jewish theme. Some common topics are: charity, kindness, observance, Torah study, prayer, the theme of any mitzvah, the nation of Israel, the land of Israel, or of course—Shabbos!

A good Torah thought is often clinched with an appropriate story. There are many books devoted to inspirational stories, and as you prepare, you will discover the ones you like best.

If you prepare well, you will find that your biggest job is to shorten your presentation to meet the needs of your audience. I recommend a time allowance of three minutes for a thought given at a typical Shabbos table. If you wish to continue longer, develop an open question which can be posed to family and guests. Then ask each person to offer his or her opinion. (Some examples appear below on pages 58-59.) I find that such questions create an interesting and enjoyable learning experience.

Following are some of my favorite Torah thoughts:

Thoughts on Prayer

Many people ask the question why must we follow a set liturgy and ask for the things outlined in the prayer book? Wouldn't it make more sense for us to simply ask G-d for what we want?

There are two types of prayer. One type contains all an individual's desires and needs—the second type of prayer contains all that we are supposed to want. This second type is personified by the prayers of the prayer book. Composed by wise sages—among them a number of prophets—our prayer book is filled with requests that should be meaningful to us. If we were to pray only on our own, we would miss out on these special prayers.

For example, a young healthy person may not think of praying for health. Our prayers remind us of what is important in life. In this way we are thankful for what we have and are reminded to pray for those who are less fortunate.

Similarly, in the liturgy of the prayer book there are requests for wisdom. It's an important request yet many people could go through life without realizing the need to make such a request. A Jew is reminded of the importance of the quest for knowledge. Indeed, there are the prayers for what each of us want, and prayers which remind each of us of what we should want.

Thoughts on Honesty

Our sages tell us that "the seal of G-d is truth."[48] Sometimes truth is a challenge, but the importance of truth cannot be overstated. Truth is applicable in many situations, but it is most often challenged in business. Honesty in business is not easy; the following parable is most instructive.

A man had a cask of wine and he installed a spigot to obtain the wine. One day he had an idea. "If instead of just one spigot," he thought, "I install two, then I would be able to obtain twice as much wine!"

Naturally, the man's reasoning was faulty since, although he would get the wine twice as fast, he cannot obtain more wine than he has in the cask.

Similarly, one who cheats in business thinks he is obtaining more money than he would have gotten otherwise. In reality, he will only get as much money as G-d wishes him to have. If he cheats, he may get it a bit faster, but in the long run, cheaters do not gain.

G-d has many ways of settling our balance. People can be hit with tremendous expenses: a few doctor bills or a broken fixture in the house. Alternatively, there are many ways that G-d can help us with saved expenses or bonus wages.

Thoughts on Observance

We have a tradition that "The ways of Torah are sweet; all of its passageways are those of peace" (Proverbs 3:17). If so, you may wonder, why don't all observant Jews enjoy their observance? Why aren't observant Jews the happiest people on earth?

A story is told of a diamond merchant who came to a hotel with a small case of diamonds. As he was checking in, a worker took the case and carried it up to the merchant's room. When the merchant got to his room, he found that the worker was panting from his exertion, and demanded a big tip. The merchant said, "If you are panting then you apparently took the wrong case. My case is very light as it is filled with diamonds."

Similarly, in observance, if one finds it difficult and heavy then he took "the wrong package." Torah is sweet; true observance is a joy. If observance is burdensome, we are doing something wrong. Perhaps our hearts aren't really in it, or perhaps we are going through a difficult phase. In its truest form, observance is a joyful experience, a way of life that is pleasurable and meant to be enjoyed.[49]

Thoughts on Persistence

The Torah in Deuteronomy 11:12 says that the land of Israel is one that "the eyes of G-d are upon it, from the beginning of *the* year until the end of *a* year." Why is it that the verse first talks of "*the* year," and then concludes by calling it "*a* year"?

Commentators explain that whenever we begin a year or any project, we think that this is going to be the year of accomplishment—the project that will really have an impact. Often, when the year is completed we realize that it was only *a* year, *a* project. It often does not reach the lofty aspirations that we had in mind.

The lesson the Torah alludes to in this verse is that even though this may be true, we must persist in our aspirations. Good intentions get us started on the right foot, but it is daily persistence that will make the ending turn out as we hoped. As King Solomon expressed it: "Better to judge things by their end than by their beginning."[50] The beginning often seems impressive. But it is the power of perseverance that makes *a* project into *the* project—an accomplishment that we can truly be proud of.

Spiritual Growth

As we grow in Torah observance, we may find ourselves confronted with new challenges. Just as we thought we finally reached a comfortable level, we may find ourselves pushed into new situations. The following parable illustrates what is happening.

When a father tries to get his child to walk, he coaxes the child to take a step. Hesitatingly, the child lets go and takes his first step. The father urges the child on, and the child slowly takes another few steps towards the father's outstretched arms. What happens when the child finally reaches his father? The father takes the child in his hands and smothers him with kisses. He holds the child lovingly and the child is content.

But what might the father do if the child was a bit more

mature? He might move his hands away from the child just as the child is about to reach him. As the child reaches the father, the father raises the goal a bit to keep the child walking. The child's goal is to be smothered with kisses and lie contentedly in his father's arms. But the father's goal is to get the child to walk. When the child reaches the initial goal, a more difficult goal takes its place.

Similarly, G-d acts like the father in the second case. Our goal is to arrive contentedly in G-d's hands. But G-d's goal is to get us to walk—to continually grow in spirituality. Therefore, once we achieve one level of observance, G-d challenges us with the next level. This is an outstanding compliment. G-d has confidence in us, and constantly urges us on to additional accomplishments.

Open Questions for Discussion

There's nothing like having a lively discussion during the Shabbos meals. Here are some open questions which can be posed at the Shabbos table. This is a good way to expand a Torah thought into meaningful discussion. Remember to choose questions that do not have a clear right and wrong answer. This way, people will be willing to offer their opinions. Don't forget to ask people to explain their answers. Naturally, the question must be prefaced with a few moments of introduction to the topic. Also, be sure to follow each question with the question "Why?"

♦ What is your favorite prayer?
♦ What do you think is G-d's favorite prayer?
♦ What is your favorite holiday?

♦ What is the best way to give charity?

♦ What is your favorite charity?

♦ What is the role of the Jewish people?

♦ What is the significance of the land of Israel?

♦ Why do good things happen to bad people?

♦ Why do bad things happen to good people?

♦ How can we unify the Jewish people?

♦ How can we ensure Jewish continuity?

♦ Why is Jewish continuity important?

♦ What is the relevance of Torah to the modern age?

Some questions may introduce differences of opinion. That is perfectly all right. Just make sure that mutual respect rules all discussions. Keep in mind that we may disagree with ideas, but must be careful to respect the people who express them.

Shabbos Afternoon

Shabbos afternoon is a special time. It offers a unique opportunity to move at a slower pace, to build relationships and relax. Long walks, napping and visiting friends are among the popular activities of Jews observing Shabbos throughout the world. In the winter the afternoons are fairly short, but in the summer, the opportunities seem endless.

Particular favorites are Shabbos parties and Shabbos study groups, invariably enhanced by refreshments. In many communities there are gatherings for both parents and children. In fact, the verse (Isaiah 58:13): And you shall call the Shabbos an *enjoyment* (the Hebrew word for enjoyment is *oneg*), is the source of the most delightful *oneg* Shabbos.

Pirkei Avos (Ethics of Our Fathers)

Taking the time to study is also a perfect activity for Shabbos afternoon. While there are lots of choices, a common topic is *Pirkei Avos* where the talmudic sages explain the Jewish value system and way of life. Shabbos is an opportunity for all types of spiritual growth. Since *Pirkei Avos* is the part of the Talmud dedicated to proper ethics, its study is most appropriate for this day. "Who is considered strong? He who possesses inner strength (4:1)," is but one of their great teachings.

Following are a few more examples of the passages found in

Pirkei Avos.

♦ "According to the difficulty, so is the reward" (5:23). Our sages viewed life's challenges a bit like exercise. The more we exert ourselves, the more effective it is. Our accomplishment is calculated according to the difficulty encountered. The more difficult a task, the more reward we have earned.

♦ "The world stands on three things: Torah, prayer and acts of kindness" (1:2). Interestingly, our forefathers each excelled in one of these three pillars. Jacob excelled in Torah study, Isaac in prayer, Abraham in kindness. These great men remain our role models for all generations.

♦ "I shall only dwell in a place of Torah" (6:9). This statement has become a slogan for Jewish communities throughout the world. To create a committed Jewish community, a Torah education is necessary. Jews who are knowledgeable in their heritage will be committed to it. The increase in education for children and adults is the type of success that we should be proud of and build upon.

The Third Meal (Shalosh Seudos)

After a relaxing afternoon, it's time for—Mincha—the short afternoon prayer service. After this we partake of the third and final Shabbos meal. Although no kiddush is recited, for many it is the highlight of Shabbos. In many communities it is eaten in the synagogue as a communal meal. We sing *Mizmor Li-Dovid*, "The Lord is my shepherd," as we bask in the final moments of Shabbos.

This third meal, also known as *Shalosh Seudos*—is traditionally a simple meal. It often includes salads, fish and other cold dishes. You may wonder why the menu is so simple for the third and final meal of Shabbos?

The story is told of a newly appointed monarch who held his inaugural banquet. The tastiest dishes were served and the general public was satiated. When the banquet was finally over, the monarch turned to his best friend and said, "Come, let us go off to the corner and spend some time with one another." So, they sat down at a table with a bit of drink and some leftover bread, enjoying each other's company.[51]

Similarly, during Shabbos we were very busy. We went to synagogue and ate two large and delicious meals. All that's left for us now is to rest. A simple menu suits us just fine. We are finally at one with G-d.

This is not to say that this third meal can't be magnificent. The point is simply that Shabbos has grown on us. We have relaxed a bit and are used to the slower pace. We don't need a gorgeous spread to convince us to relax and enjoy this special time. For these final moments of Shabbos the Jew becomes more like an angel than a human.

Psalm 23

"The Lord is my shepherd, I shall not want" (Psalm 23:1). These inspirational words, taken from Psalm 23, are commonly sung at the final Shabbos meal. As with all of King David's Psalms, it has inspired generations. David's outpouring of love, his commitment to good, has lent faith to Jews during challenging times.

In his own life David experienced many ups and downs. His confrontations with his brothers, with the Jewish King Saul, and even with his own son, left him a better person, with a clear perspective on life and its challenges. As the Psalmist, King David recognizes both good and bad as coming from G-d. Even in difficulty, he recognizes that G-d has a plan, and views G-d as his shepherd.

With this in mind, King David says, "When I settle down, it is in G-d's pasture; when I travel it is along the waters of comfort. My spirit is at ease for I know that G-d is just; all that He does is for a purpose." Circumstances do not control David's frame of mind. Happiness comes from a strong inner source. Even in difficulty David has the ability to say, "My cup runneth over."

The Psalmist never loses sight of G-d's love. "You have anointed me," with a covenant that remains strong even in difficult times. It is such inner strength that enables David to achieve serenity. He is steadfast in his awareness that his relationship with G-d has never been questioned.

On Shabbos we share in David's vision. Even the pauper among us is a prince with a G-dly mission. It is the inner strength of Shabbos that we carry throughout the week, as we pray, "May only good and kindness pursue us; may we dwell in the house of G-d until the end of days."

Mizmor LiDovid (Psalm 23)

Mizmor liDovid, Ado-noy ro-ie lo echsor. Binios deshe yarbiytzeini, al mei minuchos yinahaleini. Nafshi

yishoveiv, yancheini bimaglei tzedek limaan shimo. Gam
key eileich bigei tzalmoves lo iyra ra key Atah imodi.
Shivticho umishantecho heimo yinachamuni. Taaroch
lifonay shulchan neged tzoriroy, diyshanto bashemen
roshie kosie rivoya. Ach tov vochesed yirdifunie kol yimey
chayay, vishavtie biveis Ado-noy liorech yomim.

A psalm of David: The Lord is my shepherd, I shall not
want. In fertile pastures He causes me to rest; along waters
of comfort He guides me. My spirit is restored, as G-d
guides me in righteousness for the sake of His name.
Even as I walk in the shadow of death, I do not fear
because You are with me. Your staff and Your support
are my comfort. You prepare for me a table opposite my
oppressors, You anointed me—my cup runneth over.
Only good and kindness shall pursue me all of my life;
may I dwell in the house of G-d until the end of days.

Another favorite song is *Yedid Nefesh*, a song which describes the love relationship between us and G-d.

Yidid Nefesh
Beloved One

Yidid nefesh av harachamon
Soul's Beloved, Merciful Father,
Mishoch avdicha el ritzoneicho
draw Your servant to Your desire.
Yorutz avdicha kimo ayol
May Your servant run like a deer

Yishtachaveh el mul hadorecha
to bow before Your majesty.
Yeerav lo yididosechah
Your friendship shall be sweeter to him
minofes tzuf vichol toam.
than good foods and honey.

Hodur noeh ziv haolam
Majestic One, Beautiful One, Radiance of the universe,
Nafshie cholas ahavosecha
my soul is sick for your love.
Onoh keil noh rifoh noh loh
Please, G-d, heal her (my soul)
Biharos loh noam zivechah
by showing her the pleasantness of Your Radiance.
Oz tischazeik visisrapay
Then she will be strengthened and cured,
Vihoysoh loh simchas olam.
and she will achieve everlasting happiness.

Vosik yehemu noh rachameichoh
Faithful One, arouse Your mercy
Vichusoh noh al bein ahuvecho
and have compassion on the son of Your beloved (Abraham).
Key zeh kamoh nichsof nichsaftie
It is many years that I have yearned intensely
Liros bisiferes uzechoh
to see the Glory of Your strength.
Eileh chomdoh liybiy

This is what my heart desires;
Vichusoh noh vial tisaleim.
have compassion and do not conceal Yourself.

Higoleh noh uferos chaviyviy olay
Please reveal Yourself, my Beloved, and spread upon me
Es sukkas shilomeicho
Your shelter of peace.
Toiyr eretz mikivodechoh
May the world be illuminated with Your Glory;
Nogiloh vinismichoh boch
we will rejoice and be happy with You.
Maheir ehhov key voh moeid
Hurry, my Beloved, for the time has come;
Vichoneynu kiymey olam.
grace us as in the times of old.

Spiritual Growth

As Shabbos comes to a close we contemplate all that we have gained. Hopefully we've been rejuvenated and the inspiration of this day will fuel us in the week ahead.

Our Sages taught: If the Jewish people would keep two Shabbosos correctly, then the redemption would certainly occur.[52]

Why is it necessary to have the fulfillment of two Shabbosos? The tone of each week is the result of the Shabbos which preceded it, and each Shabbos is the result of the week which preceded it. If Shabbos is one of holiness, then it exports holiness into the week that follows. That week can, in turn, export holiness into the Shabbos that follows it. In order to create a truly spiritual Shabbos, we must first sanctify the Shabbos which precedes it. We must therefore keep two consecutive Shabbosos. It is through such preparation that we can infuse the second Shabbos with a truly spiritual quality.[53]

The Talmud teaches: "He who toils before Shabbos shall eat on Shabbos."[54] This does not refer only to the food preparations. It refers to one's spirituality and outlook on life. If one looks at Shabbos as the culmination of creation, then one's week is spent in an entirely different way and with an entirely different outlook. Each day the focus is toward Shabbos. In fact, throughout the week, we remember Shabbos as we say in our prayers, "Today is the first day to Shabbos. Today is the second day to Shabbos."[55] We constantly count toward the coming Shabbos, as we remember that we are never more than three days from a Shabbos, either the Shabbos that just passed or the Shabbos that will be.[56]

Shabbos is the focus of the entire week. This one day of rest infuses us with the strength to maximize our potential. Shabbos shows us how wonderful our lives can be.

There is a legend told of a man named Avraham who used to spend every Shabbos in the home of his Rabbi. During the week Avraham was a blacksmith, but on Shabbos he would put on his special Shabbos clothes and was accorded the greatest honors. He would sit in a prestigious seat—near the Rabbi—and everyone would greet him warmly.

But it bothered him. During the week while he worked as a blacksmith, he dressed in work clothes. On Shabbos he wore his formal fancy clothes. Somehow it bothered him to play this game. He decided that on the following Shabbos he would be totally honest and he would wear his work clothes on Shabbos.

And so he did, but Shabbos just wasn't the same. His Rabbi was clearly disappointed. Avraham was given an insignificant seat in the back of the synagogue and he suffered deeply all Shabbos. After Shabbos he approached his Rabbi to explain. He said that he was only trying to be honest with himself and with others. After all, he was only a simple blacksmith.

The Rabbi looked at him with tears in his eyes. "You think I didn't know that you were a blacksmith during the week? Of course I knew. But I thought, that wasn't the real you. That was just what you did for a living. I thought that the real you was the person I saw on Shabbos, a prestigious Jew in resplendent garments. But I see that I was mistaken. When you saw a contradiction in your personality, you chose the weekday Avraham and not the wonderful Shabbos Avraham."

Similarly, as we grow spiritually, we may begin to feel a change within ourselves. We may wonder how we will uncover our real selves. Remember, every Jew, at the core, is the essence of good. The week's distractions may cover who we really are. The special gift of Shabbos can bring happiness and comfort into our lives.

Havdalah — Farewell

Shabbos ends at nightfall on Saturday evening, which, in the United States, occurs 50 minutes after sunset.[57] Technically speaking, one is allowed to begin doing work at this time. However, the Rabbis stated that it is improper to involve oneself in other pursuits until after one has taken leave of the Shabbos.[58] The ceremony where we take leave of Shabbos is called *havdalah*.

The *havdalah* ceremony is replete with customs of mystical origin. Our traditions place the moments of *havdalah* as a particularly propitious time for prayer; it is the time when we export the spirituality of Shabbos to the entire week. It is also a time when the Almighty looks favorably upon us, and so we should take the opportunity to pray for our needs, especially for health, peace, and success.[59]

Havdalah
♦ ♦ ♦ How to do it ♦ ♦ ♦

To make *havdalah* you will need a cup, wine or grape juice, smelling spices (e.g., cloves), a *havdalah* candle (which contains at least two wicks) or two candles that can be put together for the blessing. If no wine or grape juice is available, beer may be used. You can find *havdalah* candles at Judaica stores or in many kosher groceries.

Before you begin, fill the cup with wine or grape juice. There is a custom of filling the cup until it overflows, in fulfillment of the verse, "my cup overflows" with joy.[60]

Others base this custom on the Talmudic saying, "Any house that does not spill wine like water will not see the signs of blessing."[61] Therefore, we liberally overfill the cup with wine, in order to fulfill the saying and merit the blessing.[62]

Alternatively, some commentators explain that the Talmudic saying is not a mystical formula to achieve blessing, but rather a very practical one. The phrase means that for a home to achieve blessing, the reaction to spilled expensive wine, must be the same as the reaction to spilled water. Only if a home is based on the same calm response will true blessing be achieved.

Once you have filled the cup with wine, you can proceed with *havdalah*. The *havdalah* prayer is made up of a number of small sections. The first part consists of a selection taken from the Scriptures, which describe G-d's assistance in our daily lives, and the salvation that He grants His people. Also included is a selection from the conclusion of the Purim story, "To the Jews was light, happiness, joy, and honor" (Esther 8:16). To which we add the prayer, "So may it be for us as well."

After the introductory sentences, you will recite the blessing on the wine (or grape juice) which is *"Hagofen"* (see p. 74). If beer is used, recite the blessing *"Shehakol."*

The Blessing on the Spices

Next, take the spices in your right hand and recite the blessing on them. Our Sages tell us that on Shabbos we are imbued with "an extra soul," referring to the added dimension of spirituality that we have on Shabbos.[63] With the departure of Shabbos, we lose this added dimension, and the spices are intended to revive us from the loss. Even more importantly, the spices symbolize how we yearn for the coming Shabbos.

The Blessing over Fire

Now it's time for the blessing over fire. The Medrash[64] explains that as nightfall arrived at the conclusion of the very first Shabbos, Adam was seized with fright. G-d placed the idea in Adam's mind to strike two rocks together, and in this way Adam created fire. Therefore, when our sages wished to legislate a blessing of thanksgiving for fire, they incorporated it into the *havdalah* ceremony.

It is fascinating that Adam's first experience of nightfall was at the conclusion of Shabbos. Although Adam was created on Friday, he did not experience nightfall until after Shabbos (not on Friday night). We can thus conclude that Shabbos is the essence of light, and on the first Shabbos of creation, this idea manifested itself in a very tangible way. For this reason some Jews do not wish one another a "good night" on Friday night, since the radiance of Shabbos precludes the connotations of night and darkness. Instead we wish each other a "Good Shabbos."[65]

The final blessing of *havdalah* discusses the concept of differentiation. The ability to differentiate between good and bad is a fundamental factor in man's intellectual abilities. As Jews, we must learn to differentiate between ourselves and non-Jews who do not have our added responsibilities. We must recognize that together with our responsibilities come many privileges and gifts, such as the gift of Shabbos, which we hope to enjoy for many generations.

♦ ♦ ♦ *Havdalah Quick Facts* ♦ ♦ ♦

♦ *Havdalah* means "separation" between Shabbos and the start of the new work week. It is a prayer recited after nightfall over a cup of wine or grape juice. Many scholars state that in addition to wine and grape juice one may use beer for *havdalah*.[66]

♦ When we make the blessing over fire, one custom is to close the right hand, with the thumb inside the fist. Then, expose your nails to the light of the fire and note the difference between the skin and the nail. This has Kabbalistic significance, and also ensures that you are close enough to the fire to benefit from it.[67]

♦ It is unclear whether women are obligated to perform the *havdalah* ceremony. It is therefore preferable for a woman to fulfill her (questionable) obligation of *havdalah* by listening to a man recite it. If this is impossible, then she should recite it herself, as most authorities maintain that she is obligated in *havdalah*.[68]

♦ If one must involve oneself in work immediately after nightfall, before reciting *havdalah*, one may recite the formula: "Blessed is He who differentiates between the Holy and the secular."[69] This formula serves as a temporary dispensation until one is able to recite the formal *havdalah.*[70]

♦ ♦ ♦ *Havdalah* ♦ ♦ ♦
Transliteration and Translation

***Hiney E-il yishuosie evtach viloh efchad, key ozie vizim-
ros Yoh Ado-noy vayihiy li liyshuoh. Ushiavtem mayim
bisason miymayney hayishuah. LaAdo-noy hayishuah,
al amichah birchosechah selah. Ado-noy tzivaos imonu
misgav lonu Elo-hey Yaakov selah. Ado-noy tzivaos
ashrei adom botayach boch. Ado-noy hoshiah haMelech
yaaneynu biyom koreinu. Layihudim hoyisoh orah
visimchah visason viyikar. Kein tihiyeh lanu.
Kos yishuos esah uvisheim Ado-noy ekrah.***

(Behold, G-d is my salvation, I trust, I do not fear—For
my strength is G-d, and He has saved me. You shall draw
water from the fountains of salvation. G-d saves us; it is
incumbent on us to praise Him. The G-d of hosts is with us;
the G-d of Jacob is our support. G-d of hosts, praised is the
man who trusts You. G-d saves, the King will answer us in
our time of need. To the Jews was light, happiness, joy and
honor—so may it be for us as well. A cup commemorating
salvation I shall lift and in the name of G-d I shall call.)

On wine:
***Boruch Atah Ado-noy Elo-heinu Melech haolam,
borei piri hagofen.***
(Blessed are You G-d, King of the universe,
Who created the fruit of the vine.)

On beer:
Boruch Atah Ado-noy Elo-heinu Melech haolam, shehakol nihiyeh bidvaroh.

(Blessed are You G-d, King of the universe,
Who brought about all things through His word.)

Recite the blessing over the spices, and then smell them:
Boruch Atah Ado-noy Elo-heinu Melech haolam, borei minei bisomim.

(Blessed are You G-d, King of the universe,
Who created the various spices.)

Recite the blessing over the fire:
Boruch Atah Ado-noy Elo-heinu Melech haolam, borei Meorei hoeish.

(Blessed are You G-d, King of the universe,
Who created the lights of the fire.)

Now recite the concluding blessing:
Boruch Atah Ado-noy Elo-heinu Melech haolam, hamavdil bein kodesh lichol, bein ohr lichoshech, bein Yisroel loamim, bein yom hashiviyie lisheishes yimey hamaaseh.
Boruch Atah Ado-noy hamavdil bein kodesh lichol.

(Blessed are You G-d, King of the universe, who separates
between holy and secular, between light and darkness,
between Israel and the nations, between Shabbos and the
other days of the week. Blessed are You G-d, who separates
between holy and secular.)

You now drink the wine. Some blow out the *havdalah* candle. Others have the custom to put the candle out by pouring wine over it, or by dipping the candle into the wine which overflowed.

The Moments After

The moments after Shabbos are imbued with a special sanctity. Although it is technically already a weekday, we are still living on the emotional high of the Shabbos day. The beautiful songs about Elijah the prophet, as well as the heartfelt prayers designated for this time, are a wonderful way to begin the new week.

The meal that follows Shabbos is called *Melaveh Malkah* which means "accompanying the Queen." It is with this meal that we bid farewell to Shabbos and express our yearning for its return next week. Ideally, one should eat bread at this meal. It is common practice, however, to fulfill this mitzvah with a much simpler, snack-like menu.[71]

As you look back at the Shabbos experience, recognize your accomplishment. Although you may not yet be able to follow all the laws perfectly, you have achieved something special. You have experienced the beauty and magic of Shabbos. You are a vital link in the chain of holiness that spans generations from the earliest moments of creation. Your observance has added fuel to the great light of Judaism and has added inspiration to the legacy of the Jewish people.

The Laws of Shabbos

"The Jewish people shall observe the Shabbos,
to create the Shabbos for generations
as an everlasting covenant."
(Exodus 31:16)

Introduction

Throughout Jewish history there have always been outstanding people. In each generation dedicated men and women made sure that Judaism would survive. Rabbi Shimon bar Yochai was such a person.

He was a student of the great Rabbi Akiva, who was killed by the Romans for teaching Torah (c. 136 CE, Israel). When Rabbi Shimon discovered that the Roman authorities were after him, he fled to the mountains and for twelve years lived in a cave. It was there that he authored the Zohar, the classic work of Kabbalistic thought.

When Rabbi Shimon finally emerged, he journeyed to a Jewish community where he saw the people preparing for Shabbos. Rabbi Shimon's attention focused on one particular man hurrying past him with two bunches of myrtle branches in his hand.

Rabbi Shimon stopped him and asked, "What are these fragrant branches for?"

"For Shabbos," the man responded.

"But why do you need two bundles?" Rabbi Shimon countered.

"One is for the positive aspects of Shabbos, and one is for the prohibitions."[1]

Rabbi Shimon was deeply gratified with the man's response. But what made Rabbi Shimon so happy?

The man acknowledged the two dimensions to Shabbos.

There are aspects of ritual observed through action, such as kiddush, prayer, and the Shabbos meal. This is the emotional dimension of Shabbos. It is an expression of the enthusiasm of Jewish observance. Then there are the laws of restraint, which represent an intellectual commitment to Shabbos. The man's message is that both dimensions are important.

In our generation we can readily identify with this insight. Many people perceive the laws of Shabbos only as prohibitions. They observe Shabbos, but without enthusiasm. To them the man declared, "There are two dimensions to Shabbos. They must both be present to complement one another."

But there are also many Jews who would like to observe the emotional aspects of Shabbos, and ignore the prohibitions. They enjoy kiddush, prayer and the Shabbos meal, but they don't feel ready to observe its restrictions. They can see the majesty of Shabbos, but don't understand its laws. To them the man said, "The Shabbos is one. The two dimensions of Shabbos must blend together into one cohesive unit." Only then will we behold the true radiance of Shabbos.

This is the role of the laws of Shabbos. The positive aspects of Shabbos represent the emotional strength required to accomplish great things. But we need the guidance of Jewish law to achieve greatness. The laws of Shabbos give us the focus to reach the spiritual heights for which we strive.

You may wonder, "Isn't it better for me to remain ignorant of the laws, rather than to learn about them and then not keep them fully?"

To deal with this question, let's consider the following scenario. A father walks into his children's bedroom, and asks them to please clean up the mess that they made. One child responds, "You are not my father, and you have no right to tell me what to do!" The other child responds, "You are my father, but I am not prepared to listen to you this minute. Perhaps in a few hours I will be ready to clean up as you have asked."

If you were in the father's position, which response would you prefer? Clearly, the response that acknowledges responsibility but requests a temporary reprieve, is by far the more desirable of the two. Similarly, one may not be able to change his or her lifestyle overnight, but it is certainly possible to learn the laws and slowly phase them into one's life. Step by step, it's possible to incrementally strive to fulfill the laws of Shabbos.[2]

Sometimes, the goal seems unreachable. We would do well to recall this most popular parable of Jewish literature.

A king announced that he would bestow great riches upon the person who would climb to the top of his private palace. It was known that there were only fifty flights of stairs to the palace, so many people arrived to accept the challenge. Once the actual climb began, however, the people realized that the steps were terribly steep, and soon they were too exhausted to continue to the top. One man forged ahead, and continued even after the others had given up. However, as he neared the twenty-fifth flight, even he was ready to give up. But, he thought to himself, "If the king is ready to reward the person who climbs to the top, then apparently such a thing is possible." Indeed, as he turned the corner at the halfway mark his faith was rewarded. He was astounded to see that the king had installed an escalator to enable the climbers to ascend the remaining twenty-five flights of stairs.

Similarly, in our goals of spirituality, as we climb the steep steps one by one, we are tempted to think that we will never reach the top. It helps to remember that "G-d doesn't ask the impossible from His creations."[3] It is our responsibility to try our best until Heavenly assistance "kicks in" and enables us to reach spiritual heights. Each step that we take is a step in the right direction, toward the realization of the profound spiritual dimension within us.

But how does one go about the quest for spirituality? Another classic parable offers guidance.

A great king, who was also an artist, had a son who was incapable of producing any sort of art. The king was disappointed, and declared that he would grant a generous reward to anyone who could teach his son to paint. Many artists came and went, but the prince exhibited no artistic talent.

One day an artist appeared at the castle and claimed that he could teach the prince to paint. "Give me just one hour to teach him the fundamentals, and you will soon see that he will achieve artistic greatness."

Everyone was skeptical, but the king agreed to give the man a chance.

Exactly one hour later, the prince emerged with an easel, and with great fanfare, he began to paint. At first his paint strokes seemed haphazard, but as the prince worked diligently at his painting a lovely picture emerged. Everyone praised the prince's talent and the genius of the artist who taught him.

It wasn't until later on that the artist's secret was discovered. Instead of teaching the prince to paint a picture, he had simply taught him to paint by number. He had marked the picture out in very light pencil markings, and the prince had dutifully filled in the markings. The prince never really learned art, but he had nevertheless produced a presentable picture.[4]

Similarly, it is very difficult for us to paint a picture of spirituality. We don't know the first thing about spirituality, so where could we possibly begin?

To accomplish this task, G-d gave us the instructions to produce a paint-by-number picture, namely, the Torah. Even if we don't understand the art of spirituality, we can still produce a work of art. But we must be willing to follow specific directions. In this way a human being can perfect his soul, and produce the "masterpiece" it was meant to be.

Although it is true that a little holiness is better than none at all, the true joy of Shabbos can exist only when the entire picture of Shabbos is painted properly. When we pick and choose from the laws, we create uncomfortable circumstances. Semicommitted observance can be confusing to children, and even to ourselves. Conversely, when we keep both the positive commandments and the prohibitions, we can bask in the radiance of Shabbos. As we increase our observance of the laws, we will enjoy more and more the radiance which Shabbos offers.

King David expressed this in Psalms (119:97) when he said, "I love Your Torah so much; it is my constant occupation." The Medrash explains that David's joy for Torah came from the fact that it was his constant occupation. He was so totally engrossed in Jewish observance that each mitzvah complemented the other. Wholehearted observance can result in a profound joy in Judaism.

Let us therefore "paint by number," according to the directions we were given. Shabbos is not a human invention that we can tamper with. Rather, it is the work of the Master Artist; by following G-d's directives, we can bring the holiness of Shabbos into our lives. In return, Shabbos will leave us with an internal glow that will warm us and shed light on our homes, on our families, and on all Israel.

Jewish Law

The year was 2448 from the creation of the universe. The place: the Sinai desert. In contrast to the sand dunes and barren hills, a nation stood able and ready. Since the Exodus from Egypt, they had risen to dazzling spiritual heights. United in their commitment, they stood before G-d, ready to experience the greatest revelation of all time: the giving of the Torah.

The Basics

Both the Bible and the oral law were given on Mount Sinai. Although most people are aware that the Bible was given, it is the oral law, however, that is the secret of our people. The oral law infuses Judaism with life. As Dayan Grunfeld so eloquently points out: the Oral Law is the *soul* of the Written Law.

Dayan Grunfeld quotes Rabbi Samson Raphael Hirsch (1808-1888, Germany), with regard to the oral law who said, "Centuries ago other nations took over from us what they call the "written bible"; but they could never really understand its inner meaning nor could they attain the spiritual height of Israel, because they lacked the oral tradition which is the key and the indispensable complement of the Written Law.[5]

Just as the soul of the written law is found in the oral law, the soul of Shabbos lies in thirty-nine categories in which the

Torah outlines actions prohibited on Shabbos. Each category represents a specific act of creativity which would distract us from our Shabbos rest. When we refrain from these actions we achieve the complete rest and serenity for which we strive.

In addition to the Torah prohibitions, there are Rabbinic prohibitions enacted to protect the Torah law. As you study the laws of Shabbos, you may wonder: Why are there so many Rabbinic safeguards to the laws of Shabbos?

Rabbinic legislation is based on the verse (Leviticus 18:30): "And you shall guard the Torah." This is a directive to enact legislation to protect the Torah. Such legislation guards the Torah and protects it from being violated.[6]

The question, however, is, why did they enact so many?

The Maharal (1526-1609, Prague) explains that the more precious something is, the more we guard it. This is true in our physical lives, and also in our spiritual lives. The greater the mitzvah, the more safeguards are enacted to protect it.[7] The Shabbos is so important that it has many safeguards, protecting it and declaring its sanctity.

Who's Who in Jewish Law

More important than understanding how the laws came to be, is understanding how the laws are applied in each generation. Who decides if a specific case is included in the general guidelines which the Torah provided? Who decides whether or not these laws include a specific, modern case of electronics.

To be sure, a thorough knowledge of the Talmud is necessary. But as we consider the scholars of Jewish law, we realize that there is another requirement. All of the great legal experts also had a tremendous love for the Jewish people. Their kindness and consideration for others was outstanding; this is what established their position as sages of our people.[8]

And it makes sense. The Zohar tells us, "G-d, Torah and the Jewish people are all one."[9] The ultimate relationship with Torah is achieved when one excels both in love for G-d and in love for the Jewish people. It follows that the authorities of Jewish law also excelled in their love for every Jew. It is upon the rulings of these sages that our discussions will be based.

The best example is Rabbi Yisroel Meir Kagan of Radin (1839-1933, Polish Lithuania). His classic book on daily Jewish law entitled *Mishnah Berurah*, is an ever popular book of rules. Interestingly, his first book was *Chofetz Chaim* (which is the name by which Rabbi Kagan is better known). The *Chofetz Chaim* book contains laws and essays against the practice of slander. Pages upon pages are devoted to promoting peace among his people. To speak badly of others simply had no place in the life of a man devoted to kindness.

Rabbi Kagan had a rule that no one should polish the floor of his home. To keep clean is fine. But this Rabbi was fearful that some beggar may be refused entry because the house had just been cleaned. He could not bear the thought, so he forbade his family to polish the floor.

Once, however, Rabbi Kagan arrived unexpectedly and found a member of his family polishing the floor. Astonished, he stood quietly for a few moments and then said wistfully, "If only people would spend as much time polishing their souls as they do the floor..."

Or consider Rabbi Moshe Feinstein (1895-1986, New York), the European-born Rabbi who guided American Jewry with wisdom and consideration, a man who studied the Talmud more than 200 times and knew it by heart. His scholarship was surpassed only by his sensitivity and compassion toward other Jews. One day, as he began his lecture, an unbalanced fellow walked into the study hall and began screaming at him, "Moshke... Oh Moshke..." Rabbi Feinstein had the gentlemen brought to his office where he listened to his convoluted complaints, until after an hour he succeeded in calming him. He later explained to a student he was close with, "In my youth such things would offend me. But I have worked on myself..."

Rabbi Feinstein was once asked why people love him so much. Taking but a moment to think, Rabbi Feinstein responded with a smile, "Maybe it's because I love them so much."

Another contemporary sage who stands out is Rabbi Shlomo Zalman Auerbach of Jerusalem. When he passed away in February of 1995 an estimated 300,000 people attended the funeral. Most striking was that thousands among them did not fit into his political or religious camp, they came to pay their last respects to this man whose genuine love was felt by all. No wonder his rulings in Torah, and in the laws of Shabbos in particular, are held with reverence by Jews throughout the world.

The following popular story illustrates the depth of concern that Rabbi Auerbach felt for every Jew.

Once Rabbi Auerbach needed the assistance of a certain banker to help a Jew who was in the midst of a terrible crisis.

One evening he called the banker but the banker was not in. He left a message that the matter concerned a suffering Jew, and that the banker should return the call whenever he got home, regardless of the time. Morning came, and as the man did not return the call, Rabbi Auerbach called him again. "Why didn't you return my call?" Rabbi Auerbach asked.

"Well, I got back late at night and I didn't want to disturb the Rabbi's sleep."

"And do you think," Rabbi Auerbach retorted forcefully, "that I was able to sleep while another person was suffering so?!"

Clearly, our greatest Torah scholars have the highest level of scholarship coupled and balanced by their love for every Jew. Through their rulings we are guided; from their devotion we are sustained, as we live proudly with the banner of observance that has kept the Jewish people alive throughout the ages.

The Significance Of Observing Divine Laws

As we study the laws of Shabbos, it is important that we focus on our goals. Certainly, we believe in reward and punishment. But as we strive to observe the Shabbos laws, we should also focus on the relationship that we can develop with G-d. Increased observance is the key to that profound relationship.[10]

Striving for higher levels of devotional service was a dominant theme among the Chasidic masters, among them Rabbi Levi Yitzchok of Berdichev (1740-1809, Russia).

The story is told about one Passover eve when Rabbi Levi Yitzchok announced, "I will not begin the seder until you bring me a bit of Turkish tobacco."

"But, Rabbi," his disciples objected, "Turkish tobacco is forbidden by law. Anyone found to possess forbidden imports can be immediately arrested. The government has police guarding all the marketplaces. How can you expect this of us?"

"Nevertheless," Rabbi Levi Yitzchok responded firmly, "we will not begin the seder until you obtain the Turkish tobacco."

The students went out to the market and shortly before sundown they returned with the illegal item. Rabbi Levi Yitzchok was ecstatic.

"Now," he said, "I have just one more assignment for you. Please get me a bit of bread from a Jewish home. I don't need a lot. Just a bit will do. But get me some bread from a Jewish home."

The students again protested but their Rabbi was adamant. "We will not begin the seder until you search for a Jewish-owned piece of bread."

The students exited and began their search. They knew that they would not be able to find any bread in a Jewish home on Passover (see Exodus 12:19 and 13:7 where the prohibition is outlined). Nevertheless they obediently went out to search for some Jewish-owned bread.

In each house they were greeted with the same consternation.

"Bread?! How could I possibly have bread. I disposed of all my bread this morning, before the holiday."

"But our Rabbi needs some bread! Just a little bit! Can't you find any at all? He won't start the seder without it."

One by one the Jewish townspeople slammed their doors on

the students. "Bread on Passover?! Unheard of! Imagine their foolishness to even ask."

"So, did you find me bread?" their Rabbi asked as they returned to his home.

"But Rabbi," the students complained, "how could you send us out on such an uncomfortable mission? You know very well that no bread can be found in a Jewish home once Passover begins."

"You mean you couldn't find any bread?"

"Of course not!"

"Did you check every house?"

"We walked from one end of town to the other asking for bread. We are the laughingstock of town. 'Bread in a Jewish home? How silly can you be?' "

Rabbi Levi Yitzchok smiled broadly. He raised the tobacco and said with emotion:

"Father in Heaven, look how lovingly Your children obey Your commandments. The government enforces its edicts brutally, yet look how easily I obtained this contraband tobacco. Three thousand years ago You declared at Sinai that we should have no leaven in our homes on Passover, and I couldn't get a piece of bread for any price. Look how dearly Your children respect their relationship with You!' "

If this statement is true about Passover, how much more does it apply to Shabbos! Every week, we proudly observe Shabbos with devotion and love. How beautiful it is to observe Shabbos, and to study the Divine system of its laws.

A Definition of Working

The purpose of Shabbos, as we have already discussed, is to achieve serenity and purpose in life. Shabbos produces a feeling of restfulness and helps to provide direction and purpose for all our endeavors. The question is: How is this done?

Our first clue comes from the Torah's comparison of Shabbos to the Sanctuary. The Sanctuary was an edifice of holiness erected in the Sinai desert, one year after the Exodus from Egypt. The purpose of the Sanctuary was to create a designated dwelling place for G-d's presence on earth—admist the Jews. Much like our synagogues and yeshivohs, the Sanctuary was designated as a place to seek spirituality.

The Sanctuary was built by Betzalel who was a master-architect. Our Rabbis tell us that Betzalel knew the mystical secrets of creation. Thus, in addition to creating an aesthetically magnificent edifice, he incorporated in the Sanctuary the fundamental principles of creation and Jewish life.

For example, in the Sanctuary there was a menorah, a candelabrum, as well as a table filled with special breads. The menorah was lit each evening and burned through the night. It symbolized the light of Torah which brightens our lives and helps us transcend the mundane aspects of life. The table holding the bread represented a human's physical sustenance, and was placed opposite the menorah to symbolize balance. As our sages stated: "If there is no flour there can be no Torah; if there is no Torah then the flour is worthless."[11]

In this way, the Sanctuary encapsulated many aspects of spirituality and the mission of the Jewish people. The *kiyor*, or washstand represented the cleansing process; the *aron*, or ark, housed the tablets and represented the eternal bond between G-d and the Jewish people. Each vessel in the Sanctuary had its purpose, as did the building of holiness, fashioned to house the vessels.

Interestingly, when the Torah compares Shabbos to the Sanctuary, the indication is that Shabbos is greater. After concluding the commandment to build the Sanctuary, G-d says in Exodus 31:13: "Only keep My Shabbos."

In other words, as important as the Sanctuary is, there is one condition attached to building it. *Don't build the Sanctuary on Shabbos.* This message is the founding pillar of the laws of Shabbos. The actions needed to build the Sanctuary are forbidden on Shabbos. Our oral tradition classifies these actions into thirty-nine principle categories.

These thirty-nine categories (outlined in the following chapters) are not actions of work in the conventional sense. In fact, often they are misunderstood because they don't seem to be "work" at all. Is striking a match considered "work"? Is running a hot tub for relaxation considered "work"?

It is important, therefore, to clarify that these thirty-nine categories are *not* representative of work in the conventional sense. Instead, they are actions of "physical-creativity." Thus, striking a match—as an act of physical-creativity—is forbidden (i.e., by lighting a match we create something: a fire).[12]

We use this unusual term "physical-creativity" because we are referring to *creativity*, not to work. Many forms of work (such as moving furniture around the house) may be technically permitted. Only acts of creativity are forbidden. Spiritual creativity, on the other hand, is the theme of the day. Physical-creativity accurately describes the nature of these categories.

The Sanctuary: A Microcosm of Creation

On Shabbos we rest from physical-creativity just as G-d rested from Creation on the day of Shabbos. And in this way we demonstrate our belief that G-d created the world.

You may ask, how it can be that the thirty-nine categories used in building the Sanctuary just happen to be the same actions which represent G-d's rest on the first Shabbos of Creation?

According to Rabbeinu Bachyah (c. 1340, Spain), the building of the Sanctuary imitated the acts of creativity that G-d used to create the world, "Because the Sanctuary is comparable to the creation of the world."[13]

The Sanctuary was a microcosm of G-d's Creation. The men who built the Sanctuary utilized the same mystical concepts used to create the world. In this way they imitated the "acts of creativity" that G-d used at the time of Creation.[14]

Therefore, when we wish to attest to the fact that G-d rested on the seventh day, we look to the "acts of creation" used in the Sanctuary. These acts of physical-creation are the physical manifestation of G-d's Creation.

Just as G-d rested from His acts of creation with the arrival of Shabbos, so, too, we refrain from our acts of "creation" on the day of Shabbos. By resting on the seventh day—just as G-d did—we reaffirm our belief that this world is not an accident but an intentional Creation, by a Creator, for a stated purpose.[15] It follows that on the day of Shabbos we focus on spiritual creativity and *not* on physical-creativity. Our intellectual abilities are focused on our relationship with our Creator, and on our desire to fulfill our purpose in the Creation.

The fact that we derive the thirty-nine categories from the prohibition against building the Sanctuary on Shabbos leads to a poignant insight. As lofty and altruistic as our intentions and goals may be, we still do not have permission to violate the laws of Shabbos. None of our intentions could be greater than the building of the holy Sanctuary; even there, Shabbos took precedence.

Shabbos takes precedence over the Sanctuary because without Shabbos, the Sanctuary is worthless. Jews become spiritually elevated through Shabbos, and Shabbos makes us worthy of the Sanctuary.

Conversely, the Temple in Jerusalem was destroyed when the moral caliber of the people eroded.[16] A Sanctuary or Temple that is merely an artificial display of spirituality has little place in Jewish life. Shabbos elevates us and makes us worthy of the Sanctuary.

The Command To Build a Sanctuary

The command to build the Sanctuary came soon after the

Jews sinned by building a golden calf. The purpose of the Sanctuary was to symbolize that even though the Jews had sinned, G-d would continue to dwell among them. G-d stated (Exodus 25:8), "And you shall make for Me a Sanctuary, and I will dwell within them."

Various commentaries on this verse point out that it does not say "I will dwell among them," but rather "within them." This implies that the ultimate goal is not that G-d should simply dwell in the Sanctuary but rather that through the Sanctuary, G-d's presence would become a part of every one of us. "Within them" refers to us—the Jewish people.

Today, although we no longer have the Sanctuary, we do have various replicas of it. Our synagogues and yeshivohs certainly represent the public sanctuaries of the Jewish people. But it is the Jewish home that enables us to incorporate G-d's presence into our daily lives. Our homes are a bastion for holiness. Even the mundane aspects of our homes can reflect the spirituality for which we strive.

Commentators to the Torah explain that although spirituality is very nice in theory, it is necessary to build a sanctuary to capture those ideals in real life. Only then do the ideals become part of tangible reality. The ideals of family harmony and loving relationships are wonderful in theory; our job is to bring those ideals to fruition. Shabbos is an opportune time to implement these ideals.

Shabbos is too precious a gift to spend on physically building things. Instead, on Shabbos, we are spiritually creative. Each week, when Shabbos arrives we receive a taste of the

World to Come. What exactly is the World to Come? It is the time when we will arrive at the ultimate goal of life: to bask in the light of the Divine. Shabbos is a taste of that ultimate goal.

This theme manifests itself in the thirty-nine categories of proscribed action. Each category contains actions that would distract us from the goal of Shabbos. By avoiding these categories we are spiritually in sync with the original Shabbos of G-d. Through Shabbos we come to appreciate creation.

It follows that the prohibitions are not simply restrictions. They are *guidelines* to achieving the serenity of Shabbos. When we observe Shabbos in its entirety, we experience the full spiritual warmth it represents.

Shabbos offers us a wonderful opportunity to use our minds. One of the great teachings of meditation is the tremendous power of the mind. If we would only stop distracting ourselves and concentrate, we would be amazed at the insights that would make our lives more meaningful. We are constantly inundated with static and distraction, making us forget the concept of serenity. Keep the TV off; don't answer the phone. You will be amazed at how much better you will feel.

Although there are aspects in the thirty-nine categories that are complex, (no one ever accused Jews of being superficial,) they have been detailed step by step, with relevant examples. I have made an effort to give examples both of the proscribed cases, as well as the permitted cases so that you will begin to understand the patterns involved. Join me on this spiritual odyssey …you will find that it holds the key to the Sanctuary of old, and to the sanctuary which you want your home to become.

Thirty-nine Categories

habbos observance is one of the Ten Commandments. The Ten Commandments are recorded in the Torah in the Book of Exodus, and then again in the Book of Deuteronomy. Interestingly, the Torah records the mitzvah of Shabbos slightly differently in these two places. In Exodus (20:8) the mitzvah of Shabbos is recorded as *"Remember* the day of Shabbos." In Deuteronomy (5:12), however, when the Torah reviews the Ten Commandments, the mitzvah of Shabbos is recorded as *"Guard* the day of Shabbos." What is the significance of this subtle difference?

Overview

Commentators explain that the statements of "Remember" and "Guard" are inextricably bound to one another; they are both required for a complete Shabbos experience. "Remember the day of Shabbos," refers to the positive commandments of Shabbos which create the aura of Shabbos. "Guard the day of Shabbos," refers to the actions which are prohibited on Shabbos. By refraining from these actions we guard the aura we have created.

The link between the positive actions and the prohibitions was expressed beautifully by the Talmud (Shavuos 20b), and incorporated by Rabbi Alkabetz in the first stanza of *Lecho*

Dodi. "Remember and Guard were said in one breath" by G-d. The Torah does not contradict itself by recording the commandment in Exodus with the word "Remember" and in Deuteronomy with the word "Guard." G-d said both words at once. This emphasizes how strongly linked are these two aspects of Shabbos.

The concept of "Guard" is not only a matter of restraint from the prohibited actions. To "Guard" requires strategy and preparation. It means that we get ready before Shabbos. It also requires that we study the Shabbos laws so that on Shabbos we know exactly what we are allowed to do and what we are not allowed to do. For this reason we dedicate the following sections to the prohibited actions and their practical applications.

Throughout the world, in many languages, Jews greet one another with the greeting of "Good Shabbos." They don't just mean kiddush and the Shabbos meal. A truly "Good Shabbos" includes observance of the prohibitions, thereby guarding the sanctity of Shabbos and enjoying Shabbos to its fullest.

By studying the Shabbos laws you will be able to bring complete Shabbos observance into your life. As you do, you will feel the excitement of being part of something very special. You are entering a Divine system that spans generations and is observed by Jews on every continent.

This book is only a beginning. Ideally, you will spend a Shabbos with an observant family and experience Shabbos as a true life experience. Our outline of these laws will help you get started on your own, and let you know what to expect.

To facilitate easy study of these laws, I have divided the categories in six sections: Gardening, food preparation, cloth production, leather production, miscellaneous categories, and erecting the Sanctuary.

While each section focuses on a specific process, the categories do relate to other actions as well. Cooking (#11), for example—a food preparation item—has application with regard to taking a shower with hot water (see *Question and Answer* section where the use of hot tap water on Shabbos is discussed pg. 164). It is important, therefore, to keep in mind that each of these categories represents a theme and not a specific action.

Gardening

We begin our discussion of the thirty-nine categories with the process through which berries were grown to produce the dye for the Sanctuary curtains. A similar process is used in our time to grow grain or vegetables.

This section could be summarized in one simple phrase. "Gardening is prohibited on Shabbos." Our purpose, however, is to identify the categories which prohibit gardening, and to understand the source for the prohibition of gardening. This will give us a deeper appreciation for the system of the Shabbos laws.

♦ ♦ ♦ *Category #1—Plowing* ♦ ♦ ♦

This category refers to any act that makes the ground more receptive to planting. Applications include tilling or softening the earth.

♦ ♦ ♦ *Category #2—Seeding* ♦ ♦ ♦

This refers to actions that enhance the growth of plants or trees. So if you have a garden or farm, Shabbos is not the time to water plants, transplant seedlings, or prune trees.

You may wonder about potted house plants. Strictly speaking, such plants are not subject to this category, since they are not attached to the ground. Nevertheless, the Rabbis legislated that such plants should be included in this category, since they might be confused with the Torah prohibition.[17]

♦ ♦ ♦ *Category #3—Harvesting* ♦ ♦ ♦

This includes any act which cuts a plant from its place of growth. So on Shabbos one may not pick vegetables or cut flowers. Similarly, mowing the lawn is not allowed on Shabbos. Another application of this category is the prohibition against breaking a branch off a tree, as it removes the branch from its place of growth.

♦ ♦ ♦ *Category #4—Making Bundles* ♦ ♦ ♦

This refers to making sheaves from stalks of grain, or gathering vegetables into a basket. "Apple picking" is prohibited even if you only gather the apples that have fallen to the ground and do not actually pick them. This is true even if the apples fell to the ground before Shabbos.[18]

The simple way to deal with this set of the categories is to take care of these things before or after Shabbos. General gardening should be postponed for Sunday; vegetables and flowers needed for Shabbos should be picked on Friday. This reflects a basic approach to preparing for Shabbos. We want to be 100 percent ready for Shabbos, so that when Shabbos arrives there will be no distractions.

Food Preparation

The next process in producing dyes for the Sanctuary curtains involves the steps of food preparation. These steps were necessary to process the berries which were then turned into dye. Similar steps were used to make the holy loaves that were used in the Sanctuary. In our time this process is used to make bread and other food products.

This section also introduces the important theme of appreciating gifts. Judaism sees the human being as a guest in G-d's creation; as any guest, it is proper for us to express our gratitude by saying "Thank You" for His hospitality. This theme is demonstrated by the blessings we recite before and after eating food. When G-d gives us a gift we are happy to thank Him for it.

Similarly, one of the themes of Shabbos is to acknowledge that all gifts come from G-d. All during the work week we are usually so involved in physical-creativity and productivity that we may lose sight of the role that G-d plays in our lives. To the Jew, Shabbos is a call to reality. Shabbos reminds us that without G-d's help we cannot succeed.

That is why we refrain from these actions on Shabbos. In essence, when we refrain from physical-creativity, we are acknowledging that there is a power greater than ourselves Who is really in charge. That acknowledgment, and the relationship with G-d that it creates, is similar to the relationship that results when we pray to G-d in times of trouble. In times of trouble, however, we are forced into that relationship; we are stuck and have no choice. On Shabbos, we enter the relationship voluntarily and with joy, as we seek a relationship with our Creator.

Because Shabbos expresses our appreciation for G-d's blessing, it is also a means of achieving future blessing. The Kabbalists teach that in heaven there are storehouses of blessing, waiting to be bestowed on humanity. Shabbos observance is a way of saying, "Thank You" for past blessings, and is therefore a key to future blessings. By observing the categories of food preparation, for example, we acknowledge that ultimately, our food is a blessing from G-d. Through this acknowledgment the storehouses of blessing are activated.

Food Preparation

The section of Food Preparation has seven categories:.

♦ ♦ ♦ *Category #5—Squeezing* ♦ ♦ ♦

In the Sanctuary this was the step in which the grain or berries were removed from their shell. In our time this refers to the prohibition against squeezing fruits to obtain their juice.

Wringing a garment of its liquid is prohibited on Shabbos, either because of this category or because of the category of laundering (#13).

♦ ♦ ♦ *Category #6—Winnowing* ♦ ♦ ♦

After the shell is cracked open, a thin layer of chaff remains on the kernel. In this process, this layer is removed from the grain.

This process was accomplished by throwing a mixture of grain and chaff into the air on a windy day. The wind would carry the chaff away, while the grain would fall back to the ground.

In our time an application can be found when peanuts are mixed with their chaff covering. This category prohibits us from blowing on the mixture to remove the chaff. Instead, you can remove the peanuts by hand for immediate consumption.[19]

♦ ♦ ♦ *Category #7—Selecting* ♦ ♦ ♦

Before proceeding to grind grain, undesirable particles (such as pebbles that got mixed in during the previous, winnowing process) have to be removed. The act of selecting is defined as "separating the undesired from the desired to fix or enhance the product."

This category has many practical applications, and is not limited to cases of food preparation. For example, it also applies to sorting laundry on Shabbos. Many a book has been published on this category alone. Let's take it step by step, starting with a practical example of what *is* permitted.

Think of a plate loaded with assorted cookies and consider choosing the cookie that you wish to eat. Take that cookie with your hand and bring it to your mouth. That is the perfect example of a permitted selection because it is the normal way of eating. You took what you wanted, with your hand, for immediate consumption.

Conversely, the prohibition refers to a case that does not meet these criteria. For example:

♦ You remove the undesired item (i.e., you take the unwanted cookies from the pile, thus fixing the pile for eating.)

♦ You separate the items by use of a utensil (e.g., using a sieve or slotted spoon to separate solids from liquids.)

♦ You separate the items for future use. This is true even if you are taking the desirable from the undesirable.

A common example of this last criteria is that, you may take a desired article of clothing from a laundry basket, if you want to wear it now. Conversely, choosing clothing for later use, or removing unwanted clothing, is prohibited.

A further elaboration of this category can be found in the *Question and Answer* section p. 166.

♦ ♦ ♦ *Category #8—Grinding* ♦ ♦ ♦

This refers to breaking a substance into smaller pieces. In the Sanctuary once the grain was separated, it was ground to process it into flour. Similarly, in our time we grind grain into flour before making bread.

Grinding includes any activity in which a natural product is divided into very small particles. Thus, on Shabbos it would be incorrect to dice a salad into minuscule pieces (i.e., to make an "Israeli salad"). Instead, the vegetables should be cut somewhat larger than normal.[20]

There is no problem with slicing carrots "long and thin." Since they are long, they are automatically considered large, and are not subject to this prohibition.[21]

◆ ◆ ◆ *Category #9—Sifting* ◆ ◆ ◆

This refers to separating the desirable from the undesirable by use of a utensil (e.g., a sieve). In the Sanctuary the grain was ground into flour, and then sifted. In this process, the flour is separated from the particles that were not ground properly.

This category does not include sifting that does not enhance the product. Thus, it is permissible to purify water which is already drinkable by sending it through a filter on Shabbos.[22]

◆ ◆ ◆ *Category #10—Kneading* ◆ ◆ ◆

This refers to mixing a substance with a liquid to produce a paste. Included in this category is joining flour and water, and making pudding.[23]

An interesting question involves mixing baby cereal on Shabbos. Obviously a child has to eat. Nevertheless, since baby cereal is a paste-like substance, it is best to consider the following options.

◆ Mix the powder with more liquid than is normally used. In this way, a paste is not created.

◆ Mix the mixture in an unusual manner. For example, mix the ingredients in reverse order, in two perpendicular motions rather than a circular motion, or while holding the spoon upside down. These changes remove the action from a Torah prohibition to a Rabbinic one (as it is no longer the normal, productive way to accomplish this action). Once a Rabbinic law is involved, in cases of need, there is room for leniency.[24]

♦ ♦ ♦ *Category #11—Cooking* ♦ ♦ ♦

This category is among the most important. In the Sanctuary it was the culmination of the dye production process. In our time, it is the category most closely related to the Shabbos meal. This category addresses the restrictions and permissible methods of warming food on Shabbos.

The basic definition of this category is "any activity that changes the state of a substance by use of heat." Thus cooking, frying or baking are not allowed on Shabbos.

There are also some indirect types of cooking not allowed on Shabbos. For example, food continues to cook in hot liquid even after it is removed from the fire. Our sages maintained that as long as someone can burn themselves on the liquid, it is considered hot enough to cook.[25] Thus, uncooked foods should not be placed in hot water. Similarly, we do not mix cold water with hot water because the hot water will heat the cold water.

Therefore, if you need warm water on Shabbos (to clean a baby for example, or to warm a bottle) hot water may be added slowly to cold water. In this way the cold water will become warm, but it will never become hot enough to be classified as cooking.[26]

The simplest way to have hot food on Shabbos is to put the food on the fire before Shabbos and leave it there until it is needed (e.g., chulent). Keep in mind that the Rabbis legislated that the fire should be covered so that no one will adjust the heat. The common method to do this is by buying a piece of tin, called a "*blech*." The *blech* is usually big enough to cover all four burners, but typically only one fire is left on. You can purchase a *blech* in any houseware store in a traditional Jewish neighborhood.

Technically speaking, Rabbinic legislation requires only that the fire be covered. In our time, however, since the fire is adjusted through knobs (and not by stoking the fire), it is preferable that the knobs also be covered.[27] In fact, there are specially molded *blechs* that bend to cover the knobs in the front of the stove. Or, you can simply cover the knobs with tape so that they cannot be adjusted on Shabbos.

Another method to have hot food on Shabbos is to warm it in a permissible manner. The following pointers will be helpful.

♦ Dry, fully cooked food (such as chicken or potatoes without gravy) may be rewarmed on Shabbos with some conditions. Firstly, the fire must be properly covered with a *blech*. Secondly, the food cannot be placed directly on the *blech* because that could be mistaken for cooking. Instead, we warm the food in an unusual manner. That is, we leave a covered pot of boiled water on the *blech* before Shabbos and then balance a pot on top of the first pot. You can put dry, fully cooked food into the top pot. If you leave it there for about three hours it can get quite hot and will certainly enhance the Shabbos meal.[28]

♦ Cold liquid may not be heated on Shabbos. However, if the liquid was once boiled and has been kept warm since Shabbos began, it may be moved from one place on the *blech* to another. Thus, a kettle of boiled water may be moved on the *blech* to where the fire is, provided that it remained somewhat warm the entire Shabbos.[29]

♦ Although we do not cook on Shabbos, there is a way to make tea or coffee from hot water that was prepared before Shabbos. The Rabbis maintained that if water is poured from the kettle to a cup, then from that cup to a second cup, the water does not cook. This is true even if the water is still very hot. This method of artificially cooling the water is called "using a third vessel" (i.e., the kettle, the first cup, the second cup). All ingredients necessary (i.e., tea, coffee, milk, sugar, etc.) may be added to the water that is in the second cup, even if the water is still hot.[30]

Cloth Production

he Sanctuary walls and partitions were constructed from cloth. A curtain is typically used to divide between two sections. In the Sanctuary the curtains were used to divide between the people and G-d's Divine presence. The curtains made it clear that humans could only travel until the curtains.

Nevertheless, these curtains held a beautiful and mystical message. They were woven by the people of Israel and had various pictures interwoven within them. The imprint of an eagle, for example, was prominently displayed to remind us of the verse (Exodus 19:4), "And I shall carry you, as on the wings of an eagle."[31] In this way the curtains represent both the distance between man and G-d, as well as the closeness.

This is an often repeated theme in Judaism. Although G-d is lofty, He still desires to have a personal relationship with each and every one of us. Thus, in our prayers, we often relate to G-d as a friend.[32]

This group of categories begins with the shearing of the wool, and comprises nine categories, until category twenty, where the weaving process is completed. These are the steps necessary to produce wool, and were used to create the beautiful curtains of the Sanctuary.

Look for a moment at the clothing that you are wearing. Did you ever wonder what was involved in its production? Let's consider the process, one step at a time.

Cloth Production

♦ ♦ ♦ *Category #12—Shearing* ♦ ♦ ♦

This refers to detaching something from an animal or a human. In the Sanctuary, the first step to create the cloth for the curtains was to obtain wool from the animal. Cutting hair or nails are examples of this category, as they detach something from a human.[33]

♦ ♦ ♦ *Category #13—Laundering* ♦ ♦ ♦

In the Sanctuary, after the wool was shorn from the animal, it had to be cleaned. This category prohibits laundering garments on Shabbos.

By extension of this category, since soaking an object is considered the first step in laundering it, we do not place a stained garment in water on Shabbos.

♦ ♦ ♦ *Category #14—Combing raw materials* ♦ ♦ ♦

This category has limited household application, but was the next step in producing wool for the Sanctuary curtains. If you've ever seen the fluffiness of raw wool you can imagine that something has to be done to make it into usable thread. In this process we take the wool and comb it into the soft, straight material out of which threads can be made.

Applications of this category are limited to raw materials. Combing one's hair is not included in this category. Hair combing that removes hair is included in shearing (#12).[34]

♦ ♦ ♦ *Category #15—Dyeing* ♦ ♦ ♦

This prohibits dyeing cloth or painting surfaces. In the Sanctuary this referred to the application of dye to the wool. Similarly, other methods of dyeing are included. Although you would not apply shoe polish on Shabbos, it is permitted to lightly brush off any dust that may be on your shoes.[35]

The application of lipstick presents a problem because it dyes the lips.[36] In recent years, a concept of "Shabbos makeup" has developed. One of the simplest methods involving such makeup is that it is so strong that it can be applied before Shabbos, and need not be applied again on Shabbos. Other types of "Shabbos makeup" are also available in the pharmacies of many Jewish neighborhoods.[37]

The category of dyeing does not apply to food mixtures. You may therefore mix tea concentrate into water, even though it changes the color of the water.[38]

♦ ♦ ♦ *Category #16—Spinning* ♦ ♦ ♦

Once the raw wool was dyed, it was ready to be twisted or spun into thread. This was accomplished by twisting sections of the wool, either by hand, or by use of a spinning wheel. Included in this category is the twisting of two strands to create a thread. For this reason, one may not re-twist the strands of a talis, should they become undone.[39]

The final categories of cloth production involve the weaving process. As a practical matter, the concept of weaving would apply in the form of crocheting. Tailoring or mending garments would be included, either in these categories, or in the category of sewing (#30).

♦ ♦ ♦ *Category #17—Arranging the threads* ♦ ♦ ♦ *for the weaving process*

As we prepare for the weaving process, the threads must be arranged properly on rods, so that the weaving can be done smoothly.

♦ ♦ ♦ *Category #18—Creating "botei nirin"* ♦ ♦ ♦

The concept of weaving is that every other thread goes above, then below, every cross thread. This creates the basic crisscross pattern of all garments and cloth. To facilitate this, a pulley system was developed to lift and lower the alternate threads. The part of the system that held the threads was called "*botei nirin.*"

♦ ♦ ♦ *Category #19—Weaving* ♦ ♦ ♦

The actual weaving process involved lifting the alternate threads by use of the *botei nirin* and sending a spool of thread through the separated threads. By doing this again and again you would eventually produce a bolt of cloth.

♦ ♦ ♦ *Category #20—Fixing threads* ♦ ♦ ♦

Occasionally, when cloth was produced, a part of the woven garment would have to be fixed. This category describes fixing individual threads as part of the weaving process.

This concludes the section that deals with making cloth. These categories are learned from the steps that were necessary to make the curtains for the Sanctuary. As a practical matter, these steps refer to making garments. By observing these categories, we express our appreciation for the clothes we wear.

Leather Production

hile the Sanctuary walls were made of cloth, the cover for the Sanctuary was made of animal hides. The Talmud tells us that an animal called *Tachash* was created especially so that its skins would be used to cover the Sanctuary. The *Tachash* was a colorful animal and had only one horn. Some scholars say that this animal is the source of the legend of the unicorn.[40]

This section involves the seven steps necessary to produce leather. A similar process is used to make shoes, as well as to produce tefillin (phylacteries) and their parchment.

Leather Production

♦ ♦ ♦ Category #21—Trapping ♦ ♦ ♦

This refers to capturing an animal or bird. In the Sanctuary it was necessary to catch animals so that they could later be killed to use their hides. This category prohibits trapping animals or limiting their ability to move. In a house setting, for instance, this category prohibits setting a mouse trap.[41]

This category applies only to non-domesticated animals. Domesticated animals, such as a pet dog, are not included in this category, so that, for instance, one may coax a pet into the house on Shabbos.[42]

♦ ♦ ♦ *Category #22—Slaughtering* ♦ ♦ ♦

In the Sanctuary this was the next step in the leather production process. It refers to killing or limiting the life of a living creature.

The commentaries explain that the underlying theme of this category is the concept of "taking life," which includes killing both animals and insects. Thus, on Shabbos, one cannot kill a fly or mosquito, even though it is very small. Similarly, one may not remove a live fish from a fish tank on Shabbos.[43]

Additionally, one may not wound an animal or person. Such an act causes blood to flow and is considered "taking life." For this reason we do not give blood on Shabbos (unless, of course, it is needed for a life threatening situation).[44]

♦ ♦ ♦ *Category #23—Skinning an animal* ♦ ♦ ♦

This category has limited household application. In the Sanctuary it was the next step in processing the hides. Skinning the animal involves the separation of the skin from the flesh of the animal.

♦ ♦ ♦ *Category #24—Tanning* ♦ ♦ ♦

The tanning process includes soaking the hides in a saltwater solution, smearing them with oil, and stretching them.

Included is this category is making a very salty dip for eating.[45] Other dips may involve kneading (#10) if they are made by mixing solids with a liquid to create a paste. It is therefore best to make all dips before Shabbos.

♦ ♦ ♦ *Category #25—Scraping* ♦ ♦ ♦

This category refers to scraping or smoothing a surface. In the Sanctuary, the rough spots would be smoothed from the hides so that they could be used.

Using a bar of soap is included in this category because when the soap is rubbed, you smooth over any rough spots it may have. Alternately, it may be classified as *"molid,"* a general classification for acts which change an object from a solid to a liquid.[46] Instead, we use liquid soap on Shabbos. In this way we uphold the laws of this category, yet do not compromise on proper hygiene.

Additionally, creams may not be applied by smoothing them on the skin. Instead, if you must apply cream on Shabbos, try to apply the cream without rubbing it in. If you must rub it in, you should do so in an unusual manner (i.e., backhanded) so that the Torah prohibition (of normal, constructive smoothing) has been avoided.[47]

It may seem odd that these categories should address such personal aspects of our lives as the use of soaps and creams. As Creator of the world, doesn't G-d have more important things to be concerned with?

The answer is that Judaism views the world from a unique perspective. We believe that the purpose of the Creation was so that G-d could develop a relationship with humans. It follows, therefore, that the personal aspects of Judaism are the very essence of our faith. Judaism sees G-d in a very personal way. G-d pays attention to us and wants to develop a personal relationship with every person. It is the personal aspects of observance that enable us to discover G-d in all aspects of our lives.

♦ ♦ ♦ *Category #26—Marking* ♦ ♦ ♦

In the Sanctuary before the hides were cut to shape and size, they were marked accordingly. This ensured that the cutting would be done properly, and there would be no waste. Practical applications of this category are limited. The perforation on a roll of paper towels or bathroom tissue is an example of "marking." But such marks are typically produced in the factory and not in a household setting.

Neither this category nor the following one apply to food stuffs.[48] Thus a piece of cake or bread may be cut to a specific shape, size, or thickness.

♦ ♦ ♦ *Category #27—Cutting to shape or size* ♦ ♦ ♦

In the Sanctuary this referred to the process in which a hide was cut to specific dimensions. As a practical matter, this category is not limited to the cutting of leather. On Shabbos, one may not cut leather—or anything else, like metal, wood, or paper.

A good example of "cutting to size" is cutting a sheet of paper towel from a large roll. Paper towels are perforated, based on a specific measurement. When one cuts a sheet on that perforated line, one is cutting the piece of paper towel to a specific, designated, dimension. This prohibition also applies to a roll of bathroom tissue.[49]

One way to avoid this problem is by cutting the paper towel

in a random location (i.e., not on the perforation). The problem is that this act will still fall into the category of tearing (#31).[50] Therefore, we use paper towels that were cut and totally detached before Shabbos. Similarly, in the case of bathroom tissue, you should either cut sections from the roll before Shabbos, or use a box of pre-cut tissue.

If you are stuck without pre-cut bathroom tissue, a number of solutions are suggested. The most practical solution is to tear the roll in an unusual manner, *not* on a perforation. By tearing in an unusual manner (such as with your elbow or arm) you avoid the Torah prohibition, as this is not the normal and productive manner to cut things. As such, it is only Rabbinically forbidden, and in cases of human dignity the Rabbis did not enforce their decrees.[51]

This concludes our discussion of leather production. As we have seen, although the subject of leather production may seem foreign, the concepts involved have application in daily life. The remaining two sections will discuss the miscellaneous categories needed to build the Sanctuary, and then the process of erecting the Sanctuary.

Miscellaneous Categories

he previous sections contained categories that involved processes necessary to cook, make curtains and process leather. This section is not part of a particular process, but is comprised of seven acts of creativity necessary for the building of the Sanctuary.

As we begin this section, keep in mind that the categories represent various aspects of human intellect and creativity. If an action can be done by humans but *not* by animals, then it is classified as "human creativity," as it is an action unique to humans. Thus, planting plants and harvesting them, as well as making clothes and processing hides, are classified as acts of human creativity. Likewise, lighting fires, cooking, and writing are acts unique to human beings and to their high level of intellect. We therefore refrain from these acts on Shabbos, to remind ourselves that physical-creativity cannot bring happiness. Although we have made advances in technology, which make refrigerators, washing machines and other modern appliances the norm, these inventions cannot make people happy. Serenity is achieved only through religion and self-discovery.

By stopping physical-creativity for one day, we remind ourselves of our real goal in the world. We recognize that physical advances are only a medium to achieve spiritual fulfillment. Let us now discuss the seven categories of this section.

♦ ♦ ♦ *Category #28—Tying a knot* ♦ ♦ ♦

In the Sanctuary knots were made in the construction of fishing nets. These nets were used to catch the *chilazon* fish. The blood of the *chilazon* fish was then utilized as a blue dye in the Sanctuary. This category prohibits tying a knot on Shabbos. One example of this category is, if you normally tie your garbage bag with a knot, keep in mind that you should not do so on Shabbos.

♦ ♦ ♦ *Category #29—Untying a knot* ♦ ♦ ♦

In the Sanctuary the fishing nets were made smaller or bigger as needed. This was done by untying the knots. The technical definition of this category is: If this type of knot may not be tied on Shabbos, it may not be untied either.[52]

What happens if you accidentally create a knot as you try to undo your shoelace? The definition of this category provides an interesting leniency in this case. Such a knot may be undone, since its creation did not violate the category of tying knots (as it was created accidentally).[53]

An example of untying a knot that *is* forbidden on Shabbos can be found with fruit and vegetable bags. When shopping, many people fill these plastic bags with fruits or vegetables and then knot them closed. We are not permitted to make such a knot on Shabbos, and are likewise not allowed to undo it. Instead of untying the knot you can simply rip the bag open. This is not considered tearing because it is being done in a destructive manner (see #31).

♦ ♦ ♦ *Category #30—Sewing* ♦ ♦ ♦

This involves joining two objects together by use of another medium. In the Sanctuary, the cloth curtains were sewn together with thread. This category also includes joining papers together with glue or staples.[54]

Naturally, the use of velcro, zippers, buttons, and snaps is fine. Such items are designated for opening and closing and not for permanently joining two objects.

Safety pins may be used on Shabbos. Since a safety pin is simply used as a temporary fastener, it is not included in this category.[55]

♦ ♦ ♦ *Category #31—Tearing* ♦ ♦ ♦

This involves ripping something apart for a constructive purpose. The classic example was in the Sanctuary where they tore a bad stitch in order to re-sew it. Another example is when a new book has some pages that are attached, we would want to tear apart the pages so that the book can be read properly. Such tearing is constructive, and is forbidden on Shabbos.[56]

Conversely, tearing something in a *destructive* manner does not violate the laws of this category. The emphasis here is on creativity. Therefore, acts which are done destructively are *not* included.

Even though destructive tearing is not included in this category, the Rabbis prohibited such cases so as to safeguard these laws. Therefore, paper should not be shredded on Shabbos, even for the purpose of destroying it.

In cases of necessity the Rabbis did not forbid destructive tearing. Thus, to access food for Shabbos it is permissible to tear a package. It is also permitted to open a bandage that is needed.[57]

Nevertheless, there is a general hesitancy with regard to opening packages on Shabbos. This is because some cases of tearing packages are actually considered constructive tearing. If a vessel is being created for future use (such as opening a can or box that can be reused), then this act may be considered constructive tearing, because a useful bag, box or can has been created.[58]

As a practical matter: You may open a container on Shabbos in a *destructive manner*. For example, if you have a box of tissues that was not opened before Shabbos, don't open it on the perforations, as this involves constructive tearing. Instead, cut it open from the side in a manner that is considered destructive and guarantees that the box will be thrown out after the contents are removed.[59] Also, be careful not to rip the writing on the package, since that is included in the category of erasing (#36).[60]

♦ ♦ ♦ *Category #32—Kindling a fire* ♦ ♦ ♦

In the Sanctuary it was necessary to use fire to cook, as well as to form the metal of the beams that held up the curtains. This category refers to starting a fire or adding to an existing fire. Thus on Shabbos, one may not strike a match, turn on a stove or oven, or add oil to a burning wick. If you were to use the fire for cooking, category #11 (cooking) would also come into play.

Additionally, it is forbidden to switch on a light on Shabbos. The authorities explain that electricity is considered the fuel, which feeds the "wick" inside the bulb. By turning the switch on, we are adding fuel, or "kindling" the light bulb.[61] Alternatively, a switch can be classified as a form of building (#37) as it completes the circuit.

One way to have the lights turned on and off on Shabbos is to set electric timers before Shabbos. These "Shabbos clocks," as they are commonly called, can switch the lights off for the night, and switch them on again for the next day. Since the lights and timers are set before Shabbos begins, and it all occurs automatically without your involvement, no forbidden action is done on Shabbos. In this way the convenience of electric lights can be enjoyed on Shabbos.[62]

This category emphasizes that it is not "work" that is forbidden on Shabbos but rather creativity. It doesn't take much effort to strike a match or flip a switch, but such an action is creative—through it light is created.

♦ ♦ ♦ *Category #33—Extinguishing a fire* ♦ ♦ ♦

This category involves any activity which limits or extinguishes a fire for a constructive purpose. In the Sanctuary, it was necessary to put out a fire in order to produce charcoal. Charcoal gives off more heat than a regular fire and would be used to heat the metals used in the Sanctuary.

Extinguishing a fire so that it should not destroy one's belongings is not forbidden by Torah law, since the intent of the firefighter is to stop the fire, and not to create something else.[63]

There is, however, a Rabbinic legislation prohibiting extinguishing a fire for a non-creative purpose. As a practical matter, however, a house fire is generally classified as endangering life—even if all the inhabitants are evacuated, there is still fear that someone may have been forgotten inside. Additionally, there is danger that the fire will spread and endanger other lives.

Therefore, if it is possible to place the burning item in a place where it can safely burn itself out (e.g., into the sink), this is preferred. Otherwise you should put out the fire or call the fire department.[64] Although using a phone on Shabbos is normally forbidden (as discussed in the act of completion, #34), cases of danger supersede Shabbos laws. This is because the Torah says (Leviticus 18:5) "And you shall *live* through the commandments," and not, G-d forbid, the opposite.

♦ ♦ ♦ *Category #34—The act of completion* ♦ ♦ ♦

In the Sanctuary the act of completion referred to the final hammer blow which completed metal construction. In our time this category includes any act which finishes or completes a manufactured article.

One example of this category is putting new laces into a pair of shoes. Since these shoes were unusable without the laces, the act of putting laces in them is considered to complete the shoe and is not allowed on Shabbos. It is, however, permitted to restore a shoelace that has slipped out.

It is also permitted to put a new shoelace into a used shoe, provided that the shoelace is a different color or you do not thread it properly. Since it will have to be redone after Shabbos, it is considered a temporary solution and is permitted.[65]

Another application of this category is electronics. Although all scholars agree that the use of electrical appliances is forbidden on Shabbos, authorities differ as to the source of this prohibition. Many authorities categorize electronic appliances as an act of completion, as the appliance is unusable until the electricity is turned on. Others say that the proper categorization for electrical appliances is building (#37) and completing an electrical circuit. Still others maintain that electricity has the same laws as fire; its use is akin to kindling a fire (#32).[66]

Unplugging an appliance would be classified in the category of extinguishing a fire (#33) or in the category of demolishing (#38), the category that refers to the removal of something from a building or to an act which makes an object unusable.

As a result of these laws, we do not turn on or off any electrical appliances on Shabbos. This refers to the use of all appliances including electric mixers, vacuum cleaners, electronic tools and telephones. If you are worried that an emergency call might come in, leave an answering machine on so that the person can leave a message for you to hear.

This concludes our discussion of categories needed to build the Sanctuary. The following section deals with the categories involved in the final erecting and in the dismantling of the Sanctuary as the Jews traveled through the desert.

Erecting the Sanctuary

The Sanctuary was a temporary structure erected and dismantled as the Jews traveled in the desert during the years following the Exodus from Egypt. The Jews were never sure how long they would stay in any one place. When the Divine order was given to travel, they would dismantle the Sanctuary and move to their next destination.

According to the commentators, the events in the desert symbolized future events in Jewish history. In each exile that the Jews experienced they were always unsure of how long their newest settlement would last. Yet, gaining inspiration from the Sanctuary of old, the Jews always built their communal sanctuary. Later, when new travel orders were given, Jewish communities moved on and erected their sanctuary in a new location.[67]

Erecting the Sanctuary

The five categories that follow were all necessary for erecting and dismantling the Sanctuary. In our time, these actions are common in construction and in home improvement projects.

♦ ♦ ♦ Category #35—Writing ♦ ♦ ♦

This category involves recording a letter or symbol on a surface. The act of writing represents the height of human creativity: the development of communication. When the Jews traveled in the desert they had to dismantle the Sanctuary and then reconstruct it at the next encampment. To make sure that the beams used to erect the Sanctuary would not be mixed up, they were marked systematically with letters. In this way, the order of the beams would remain the same, thus ensuring, that the hand-crafted beams would nest together properly, and that the beams designated for the holiest part of the Sanctuary would not be switched to a lesser degree of holiness.

Writing with a pen or pencil is included in this category, as is the use of a typewriter. Typing on a computer would also be included, because the letters that are created remain in place until they are actively erased.[68] Painting a picture would be included in this category, or in the category of dyeing (#15).[69]

As an extension of the category of writing, the Rabbis legislated a prohibition against all business dealings. They maintained that such dealings were usually recorded and would bring to a violation of the laws of Shabbos. Additionally, by prohibiting business dealings, the Rabbis complemented the philosophical principles of Shabbos. On Shabbos we leave the cares of the work week behind and trust in G-d that our needs will be provided for.

The prohibition against doing business on Shabbos is also very helpful in our quest for self-discovery. Too often, we define ourselves by what we do and not by who we really are. "I am a lawyer; I am an accountant; I am an electrician" describes one's occupation, but does not define the essence of one's self. Shabbos comes to assist us in proper self-definition. On Shabbos we refrain from business and instead focus on family, friends and spirituality. Shabbos enables us to discover who we really are.

♦ ♦ ♦ *Category #36—Erasing* ♦ ♦ ♦

In the Sanctuary there were times that a designated marking on a beam had to be changed and corrected. To do this, the original marking was erased. Erasing for a constructive purpose represents a great accomplishment, an accomplishment comparable to writing itself. It represents the ability to correct a mistake, and thereby start the writing process anew.

In its classic sense erasing refers to the erasing of letters to create a clean place for writing. Additionally, there is a Rabbinic prohibition against destroying letters on Shabbos, even if a clean place was not created.[70]

It is permitted to break a biscuit or chocolate bar that has lettering molded into it, since such lettering is considered part of the food, and is not considered a separate entity.[71] If, however, the letters were added on, (such as in the case of a birthday cake,) then you should not cut the letters on Shabbos. In such cases, a number of solutions should be considered. You might want to cut the cake before Shabbos, or on Shabbos cut the cake between the letters. Alternatively, you may put a thin layer of cardboard or chocolate on the cake before applying the decorative top. In this way the decorative top with lettering can be removed on Shabbos, and the cake can be eaten, while the decorative top could be saved for after Shabbos.[72]

♦ ♦ ♦ *Category #37 Building* ♦ ♦ ♦

This prohibits acts of construction on Shabbos. The Sanctuary was erected by connecting the beams and then covering them with curtains. Any act that adds to a building or creates furniture would be included in this category. Thus, home improvement plans should be postponed until Sunday.

It is permissible to open windows or doors on Shabbos since they are both on hinges, and this movement is considered their normal method of use.

♦ ♦ ♦ *Category #38—Demolishing* ♦ ♦ ♦

This category prohibits demolition that is done for a constructive purpose. The beams of the Sanctuary were dismantled when the Jews traveled from place to place. In our time ripping out cabinets so as to replace them would be an example of constructive demolition. There is a Rabbinic legislation against destructive demolition. Simply said, we do not break things on Shabbos.

♦ ♦ ♦ *Category #39—Transfer* [73] ♦ ♦ ♦

This is the final and probably the most fascinating category. It refers to the act of transferring (or carrying) an object from one place to another. In the Sanctuary it was necessary to transport the beams from place to place. The classic example of this category is carrying an object from a private area (like your house) to the public area (the street).[74]

Another example is carrying an object four cubits (about six feet) in the public area. Thus, we do not carry things in our hands or pockets when we walk outside on Shabbos. It is, however, permitted to wear jewelry and clothing.[75]

One of the important issues which this category raises is how to carry the key to your house. Many innovative solutions exist. Some people make a tie clip or decorative pin with their key. This allows them to wear it on Shabbos as a piece of jewelry. Others incorporate the key as a link in a bracelet or as a clasp on their belt. Still, for some people, the best solution is to install a non-electric push button combination lock. This enables you to lock your house and then get in without using a key at all.

Many communities have built an *eiruv*. This is an enclosure around the city which gives the entire area the status of one big private area. Under such circumstances you would be allowed to carry in what would seem to be the public area.

This category emphasizes that the concept of work on Shabbos is not based on its physical representation, but rather how we look at it conceptually. The act of transfer from one domain to another can be as easy as carrying a garment in your hand. Certainly, we would not consider this work.

Nevertheless, the ability to transfer from one domain to another represents the intellectual root of a civilized society. Transfer is the concept upon which all of commerce and human relations are based, and is therefore considered an act of physical-creativity.[76]

Additionally, by forbidding transfer on Shabbos, the Torah forces us to prepare properly for Shabbos. Everything we need must be placed in its proper location before Shabbos.[77] In this way we guarantee that when Shabbos arrives we are ready to emphasize the spiritual-creativity which this day personifies.

Conclusion

This concludes our discussion of the categories. I have attempted to outline the theme and logic of these laws. Naturally, this is just an introductory guide and does not cover everything. If you have a personal problem, visit a Rabbi and explain the details of your case.

Also, remember that although Judaism emphasizes scholarship, it is essentially *not* an academic study but rather a way of life. As such, successful and fulfilling observance can be achieved only by experiencing Shabbos, and through personal consultation with a capable and understanding guide.

Muktza

uktza is a Hebrew word which means "set aside." It refers to objects that are not intended to be used on Shabbos and are therefore considered off limits. Examples include: a hammer, a pen, money, stones, musical instruments, and a variety of similar objects not generally used on Shabbos.

Our Rabbis based the concept of *muktza* on the verse in Isaiah (58:13) which tells us: "and you shall honor Shabbos by refraining from your tasks and from improper speech." Our Rabbis inferred that if G-d wants our speech on Shabbos to be more refined than our speech throughout the week, then certainly the items we handle should reflect the sanctity of the day.[78] The Rabbis therefore enacted the laws of *muktza*, which state: "On Shabbos, one should not handle an item not prepared for Shabbos use."

Interestingly enough, the Talmud tells us that there was a time that the laws of *muktza* were much more stringent than they are today. At the time that the Second Jewish Commonwealth began (c. 350 BCE) the terrible decline of the Jewish communities was evident. As we read in the Book of Nehemiah (13:15, 23) many of the Jews had intermarried, and were not observing the Shabbos properly. Business people could be found in the marketplace on this holy day, and the sanctity of Shabbos was unfamiliar to too many Jews. (Sound familiar?)

At that time, the great Jewish leader Nehemiah rallied the Jews together and inspired them to rededicate themselves to Jewish life.[79] They separated from their non-Jewish spouses, and committed themselves to building the Jewish people.

In order to strengthen the observance of Shabbos the Rabbis initiated a series of enactments with regard to the laws of *muktza*. They said, "It is possible for people to technically observe the laws of Shabbos, and nevertheless be involved in other pursuits the entire day."[80] Therefore, they enacted the laws of *muktza* with such stringency that almost anything not needed for Shabbos observance was deemed *muktza*. Eventually, as the observance of Shabbos once again became the norm among the Jews, the Rabbis abolished the extremely stringent part of the *muktza* laws. The limited number of restricted items that remained comprise the categories of *muktza* applicable today.

Because it takes time to understand the concept of *muktza*, we will stick to the four most common cases.[81] They will first be defined, then practical questions will be discussed.

Four Most Common Categories of Muktza

A) The first and simplest category is called "things which are normally used for a **permitted purpose**." This category includes such items as cutlery, bowls, chairs, clothing, and food products. These items may be moved for any reason at all.[82]

B) The second category of *muktza* is called "things which are normally used for a **forbidden purpose**." This category includes things like a hammer, a pen, and gardening tools. Since such items are normally used for purposes that are forbidden on Shabbos, the following restrictions apply to them.

♦ Such items may not be moved to protect the item itself. For example: if you left a hammer outside, it is not possible to move it during Shabbos to prevent it from being stolen or ruined by the rain.

♦ Such items may be moved and used only if they are needed for a permitted use. For example: if one needs a hammer to crack open a coconut, it may be used.

♦ Similarly, it is permitted to move such an item if it is in the way. For example: if a hammer was left on the Shabbos table, it may be removed and placed elsewhere.[83]

The guiding rule of this category is that if the movement is for *the benefit of the forbidden item,* it may not be moved. If, however, the movement is for a permitted use of the object, or to use the place of the object, it may be moved.

C) The third category of *muktza* involves objects that are **unprepared** for use. This category includes rocks, sand, and twigs. These objects were never designated for use, and are by their very nature unprepared for use.

If such objects are designated for use before Shabbos, they may be moved. For example, one may designate a specific rock as a paperweight. Similarly, one may designate a bucket of sand for use on an icy walkway.[84] Once these items are designated for use, they may be used on Shabbos.

D) The fourth category of *muktza* involves the **base** that supports a *muktza* object.[85] Examples of this would be a tray that supports Shabbos candlesticks. Also included would be a drawer in which *muktza* items are stored.

An interesting addendum to this is that the base is *muktza* if it is supporting *only* the *muktza* item. If, however, when Shabbos began, the base also supported a permitted item of greater value, then the base does not become *muktza*.[86] For this reason, a drawer will usually not become *muktza*, since it contains permitted items of greater value than the *muktza* item. Thus, in most cases, a drawer may be opened on Shabbos.

Since *muktza* is a difficult concept, let's now focus on some practical questions that may arise with regard to these laws.

Questions and Answers Regarding Muktza

Question: *After removing the chulent from the crockpot, you decide that you would like more space on the counter to serve the chulent. Are you allowed to push the crockpot to the side of the counter?*

Answer: The crockpot is a vessel used to cook things. Since cooking is forbidden on Shabbos, the pot is deemed an object that has a forbidden use (category B). As such, you may move it to make use of the space that it is occupying. While moving the crockpot, care should be taken not to remove the plug.

Question: *Late on Friday afternoon you realize that although you bought walnuts for Shabbos you don't have a nutcracker to crack them with. You decide to take a rock from outside to designate as your nutcracker. May you do so?*

Answer: A rock is something that is *muktza* because it is unprepared (category C). As such, once it is designated for use before Shabbos, it may be used on Shabbos.

There is, however, a disagreement among Rabbinical authorities as to what exactly constitutes designation. Preferably, the item should either be designated for permanent use, or an action should be done to make it more usable for its designated use.[87] In the case of a rock, you should scrape it in some way (with a different rock, or on the concrete) in order to officially designate it for Shabbos use.

Question: *The Shabbos candles have been lit in candlesticks placed on the Shabbos table. Now that the meal is over, and the candles have burnt out, you'd like to move the table.[88] Is it possible?*

Answer: Our initial reaction would be that the table has become a base (category D) to the candles which are *muktza*. If so, it would be forbidden to move the table. The Shabbos table, however, does not follow this ruling. Many Rabbinical authorities maintain that the Shabbos challohs are so important that they are considered to be of greater value than the *muktza* objects. Therefore, if the challohs are on the table when Shabbos begins, the table will not become a base to the candlesticks. Since the table supports the challah (i.e., a non-*muktza* object), it is not considered a base for the *muktza* item. As such, the table may be moved after the candles go out.[89]

Question: *Your battery-operated alarm clock was not shut off before Shabbos, and on Shabbos morning it rings loudly. You'd like to move it to a different room so that you can go back to sleep. May you do so?*

Answer: Certainly! The alarm clock is an electronic device which you cannot "use" (i.e., activate or deactivate) on Shabbos. As such, it may be classified as "an item with a forbidden use" (category B) and may be moved if it is in the way. In our case, it is considered "in the way" because in this room it is hindering your sleep.[90]

It is also permitted to move the clock so that the time can be more easily seen. This is an example of moving a *muktza* item for a permitted use. Care should be taken not to touch any of the switches or buttons.

Question: *While clearing the table, a glass drops and breaks. Is it permitted to clean up the pieces on Shabbos?*

Answer: Theoretically, there are *muktza* restrictions that apply to thin shards of glass. Since they have no present use, they might be considered *muktza*. It might be preferable to kick the glass into a safe place, instead of actually picking it up by hand.

As a practical matter, however, the glass is considered a danger to those in the house, particularly if there are children around. As such, the shards of glass may be carefully moved by hand because in cases of danger, the laws of *muktza* do not apply.[91]

Note: A *muktza* item may be kicked, or pushed with one's elbow. Such abnormal movement is not subject to the laws of *muktza*.[92]

Of all the laws of Shabbos, it is *muktza* that demonstrates the uniqueness of this day. Not only do we observe the laws, we don't even handle objects that could violate the sanctity of the day. The following story illustrates the powerful message that the laws of *muktza* can send to children about the sanctity of Shabbos.

Yitzchak was an eight-year-old boy who grew up in Jerusalem in the early 1900's.

One Shabbos, as he headed for the Western Wall, he noticed a gold coin on the sidewalk, a coin so valuable that it could support his family for two weeks. But it was Shabbos, and he couldn't pick it up. Instead, a determined Yitzchak decided to stand on the coin until Shabbos would be over and he could finally take it home.

After an hour of standing still, an Arab youth approached him. "Why don't you move on?" he asked. "Why are you standing there like a statue?"

At first, Yitzchak didn't answer. But when the larger and stronger boy persisted, he replied innocently, "I have something under my foot that I can't pick up today because it is Shabbos. I'm watching it so that after Shabbos I..."

Before Yitzchak could finish his sentence, the Arab boy shoved him to the ground and ran off with the coin. A stunned and dejected Yitzchak lay in the street, which is how the Chernobyler Rebbe found him. The Rebbe saw how upset Yitzchak was and listened to him recount what had happened. "Come to my home after Shabbos," he told Yitzchak. "We'll discuss it then."

In the Rebbe's home that night the Rebbe showed Yitzchak a gold coin identical to the one he had lost. "Here, this is yours because you didn't pick up the *muktza* coin this afternoon," he told Yitzchak. "But there is one condition: I get the reward for your mitzvah."

Little Yitzchak gazed at the coin and envisioned all that it could buy; he was amazed. Was his respect for the laws of *muktza* really worth this beautiful gold coin?

It took Yitzchak but a moment to compose his response. "If that is what the mitzvah is worth," he said softly, "then the mitzvah is not for sale."[93]

On Jewish Continuity

We have discussed how we learned the thirty-nine categories from the building of the Sanctuary (see pp. 92-95). The comparison of Shabbos to the Sanctuary doesn't end there. The holiness created through the Sanctuary is the same holiness that we create through Shabbos observance. In fact, the observance of Shabbos is greater than the Sanctuary in three respects.

When building the Sanctuary, it was necessary to perform thirty-nine types of creative activity. In contrast, the holiness of Shabbos is created by *refraining* from such actions. There is no need for us to create the holiness of Shabbos, because G-d has already blessed it from the time of creation. All that we have to do is prepare ourselves to reap its benefits.

When the Jews built the Sanctuary, they were not guaranteed that G-d would rest His presence in their handiwork. In contrast, the Shabbos was granted as a gift to the Jews. If we put effort into observing Shabbos, we are guaranteed results.

In addition, the Sanctuary was only able to be built in a designated place, first in the desert and then in Jerusalem. Shabbos, on the other hand, goes wherever we do, infusing us with the holiness needed to survive the turmoil of exile. It has been wisely stated: More than the Jewish people have guarded the Shabbos, the Shabbos has guarded the Jewish people.

In our generation, the great buzzword on the Jewish agenda is Jewish continuity. We would like to successfully perpetuate our traditions to a new generation. Herculean efforts have been expended in this area, and yet we cannot truly say that the tide has turned. Nonetheless, the historic destiny of Judaism can be a great source of hope.

As the Jews have wandered from land to land the Torah nurtured them. In Spain in 1492 when the Jews were expelled or forced to convert, in Germany in 1942 during the horrific "final solution," it was the Torah that gave the Jews the strength to carry on. That same Torah can infuse us with the vitality to continue if we will only listen to its words. For it is the Torah and its mitzvohs that hold the secret of Jewish survival, as Moses exhorts the Jewish people prior to his passing:

"Look, I have set before you life and good, and death and bad...And you shall choose life."[94] Shabbos is foremost among the mitzvohs. Because Shabbos is much more than a simple tradition. Shabbos is the essence of our faith. A Jew who observes Shabbos is a *practicing* Jew; a Jew who does not is missing the heartbeat of his or her people.

But continuity is not limited to Shabbos. The key to Jewish continuity is Jewish education. We must ensure that our children are properly educated in Jewish law and tradition. They must be shown the beauty of our traditions and the magnificence of our people. This is the pivotal role of the yeshiva day school; through it Jewish continuity can be achieved. For if parents desire their children to be dedicated Jews without being knowledgeable in Judaism, then they are trying to produce something that never was and never will be. Only education can produce dedication.

For more information regarding some of the educational possibilities and books presently available see pages 147-156. You'll find there many ways to rejuvenate the spirit of Israel, and rededicate ourselves to our wonderful heritage. Our goal is to kindle the Shabbos lights and rekindle the lights of Jewish youth. I pray to G-d that He enable us to do so.

In Conclusion

Shabbos can be understood and appreciated on many different levels. It is a family day and a day of spirituality. It is a day to slow down and enjoy life, as well as a day to express our appreciation for G-d's blessings. Shabbos is not only a covenant of old. It is also a covenant of youth, intended for those who seek meaning in life.

Shabbos achieves all this through its two dimensions. Shabbos is exuberance. This is achieved through kiddush and the Shabbos meal. Shabbos is also a way of life, as displayed by the way the laws of Shabbos guide us through this day.

In this book we have outlined many aspects of Shabbos from an intellectual perspective. Ultimately, however, Shabbos can be appreciated only through real life experience. An authentic Shabbos experience can illustrate Shabbos better than any book.

A real Shabbos experience requires flexibility. To those raised in religious homes, the dos and don'ts come naturally. But for the beginner, Shabbos requires an effort to change. When you visit different homes you will notice various customs. Watch and see, experience and learn. Accepting too much, too fast can be counterproductive. But participation and slow, steady spiritual growth can phase the gift of Shabbos into your life.

The laws against using electronic appliances on Shabbos are often the most difficult to get used to. For example, the lights must be turned on or off before Shabbos, or timers set before

Shabbos to turn them on or off as needed. In many homes, the light switches are covered with tape, metal, velcro or magnetic covers so that they will not be adjusted on Shabbos.

If you live with Jews who have not yet been turned on to Shabbos observance, things may not be so easy. Your new-found religious zeal is important to you, but may not be shared by other family members. Unscrewing the light in the refrigerator before Shabbos (so that you can open the refrigerator on Shabbos without turning on the light) is just one common example of a delicate area that may require negotiation.

It is best to approach these situations with sensitivity and understanding. Don't impose your religious standards on other people. Instead, ask for their consideration in achieving the goals that are meaningful to you. Experience has shown that people will be willing to do almost anything to preserve a friendly and loving relationship.

I close with my fondest and most sincere best wishes. Each step in Shabbos observance is a monumentally significant one. May G-d bless you and help you to continue to grow and accomplish all that is good. May G-d assist you in all that you do, and bless you with the blessings of Shabbos for all time. Shalom!

Opportunities for Study

In response to the common question "How can I further my Jewish education?" I have compiled a list of seminars, books and tapes.

Introduction to Judaism Seminars and Study Groups

♦ The Discovery Seminars are popular throughout North America. A full exposition of Jewish thought and history is presented in workshops and lectures. "Why do Jews hang on steadfastly to a religion that is three thousand years old?" "Is it true that the Torah is Divine?" These and other questions are examined and discussed. For more information, contact Discovery at 718-376-2775. Internet address: http://www.discoveryseminar.org.

A similar program, Gateways, can be reached by calling 800-772-3191 or 914-356-2766. They are particularly oriented to weekend, vacation-like seminars.

♦ The National Jewish Outreach Programs (NJOP), has developed a course through which Hebrew reading can be taught in five sessions. This course is taught in synagogues and community centers throughout the United States. For more information about this, or their Basic Judaism Crash Course, call NJOP at 800-44 HEBRE(W). Internet address: http://www.hjop.org.

♦ The Orthodox Union (OU) has begun monthly interactive

study groups around the country. Materials used to stimulate the discussions are compiled by the Pardes team, who build bridges between traditional Torah sources and daily life. Audience participation makes these groups a wonderful forum for exchanging ideas. To find a group near you, call 800-4 Chaver, or 212-563-4000. Internet address: http://www.ou.org/pardes.

♦ "Partners in Torah" study sessions bring Jews of varied backgrounds together with student scholars of a local yeshiva. Call 212-227-1000.

An innovative program entitled Project SEED has been organized for communities without a local yeshiva to accommodate Partners in Torah. Project SEED is scheduled during the school summer break. Yeshiva students travel to various communities that are interested in learning more about Judaism. This program includes one-on-one learning as well as lectures. Topics include: Talmud, Bible, holidays, mysticism, and Jewish law.

For more information on Partners in Torah or Project SEED contact the Torah Umesorah office at 212-227-1000. Torah Umesorah is also a guidance network for Jewish day schools, and can be helpful in locating a day school in your area.

♦ Many schools for adults exist, both in the United States and in Israel. In the U.S., contact Ohr Somayach at 914-425-1370, or 1-800-OHR SOMA (YACH). Located in the foothills of the Catskill Mountains, Ohr Somayach has successfully blended the joys of Jewish education with an enjoyable recreational experience. Internet address: http://www.legacynet.org/. Ohr Somayach has a large branch in Jerusalem as well. POB

18103, Jerusalem Israel 91180. Phone: [011 972 2] 581-0315. Fax: 581-2890.

Aish HaTorah is another exciting program which offers a comprehensive blend of learning and touring Israel as well as Shabbos gatherings in many synagogues. The main branch is in Israel, located at 1 Western Wall Plaza, POB 14149, Old City Jerusalem, Israel. Alternatively you can call the Heritage House at (02) 627-1916, or Aish HaTorah at (02) 628-5666. Fax: (from U.S.) 011-972-2-627-3172. Internet address: http://www.aish.edu/essentials.

Among the Aish HaTorah branches in the U.S. are:

Cleveland, OH, 216-321-7277; Detroit, MI, 810-737-0400; Los Angeles CA, 310-278-8672; Miami, FL, 305-945-2155; Monsey, NY, 914-425-7040; New York, NY, 212-579-1388.

Audio Tapes

One great way to enjoy learning is by listening to audio tapes. Music tapes offer an important social aspect of Judaism. Lecture tapes are great for traveling and for relaxed study.

♦ *Journeys 1* and *2* as well as *Destiny 1*, are tapes composed almost entirely of English lyrics. I also recommend *A Taste of Shabbos*, Shabbos songs with English narration.

♦ Rabbi Berel Wein's highly acclaimed Jewish history series brings such times as King David's rule, Maimonides' time, the State of Israel, and the Six Day War vividly alive. A complete catalog is available through Shaar Communications: 1-800-499-WEIN. Fax: 914-356-7733.

♦ Rabbi Noah Weinberg of Aish HaTorah has recorded a

popular series entitled *48 Ways to Wisdom*. Using traditional Jewish techniques, Rabbi Weinberg has transformed the difficult task of self-improvement into an enjoyable and productive experience. Also available from Aish HaTorah is a tape of Shabbos songs. A catalog can be obtained by writing: Aish HaTorah Audio Center, 4 Haven Court, Monsey, N.Y. 10952, or call 1-800-VOICES-3.

Book Publishers and Distributors

The following is a list of three popular publishers of Judaica. Each has full catalogs that they will send without cost.

♦ The Judaica Press
123 Ditmas Avenue
Brooklyn NY 11218
718-972-6200 or 1-800-972-6201

♦ Artscroll-Mesorah Publications
4401 Second Avenue
Brooklyn NY 11232
718-921-9000 or 1-800-MESORAH

♦ Feldheim Publishers
200 Airport Executive Park
Nanuet NY 10954
914-356-2282 or 1-800-237-7149

♦ Most Judaica stores will ship any item, and the salespeople at the stores can recommend books to suit your interests. Among them:

- Goldman's Judaica Outlet 718-972-6200
  or 1-800-972-6201
- Judaica Express, 1-800-2 BOOKS 1
- Tuvia's, 914-426-0824
- Eichler's 718-258-7643 or 1-800-883-4245

Internet Sites

The Internet has become an interesting source of information. The following Internet sites are good starting points. Many provide links to discussion groups and many Jewish services.

OU, NCSY, kosher products and a national network of congregations and contacts: HTTP://www.ou.org.

Project Genesis, all types of Torah discussion. A happening place: HTTP://www.torah.org/

Kashrut.com, information about kosher food. Also provides good links, including a program for sunrise and sunset in different cities.

The homepage for Aish HaTorah in Jerusalem and the world wide Discovery seminars: Aish.org

Great links: Virtual.co.il, Thewall.org, shemayisroel.co.il.

Additional Contacts

For one-on-one study sessions over the phone, contact Partners in Torah at 1-800-STUDY 4 2. They will arrange for a weekly phone study session on the topic of your choice.

If you have questions about Judaism that you would like to discuss, you can contact a Jewish educator in your area. Write or call the Association for Jewish Outreach Professionals

(AJOP) at 3 West 16th St., New York, NY 10011, 212-929-1525 ext. 285 or ext. 286.

Specific Shabbos Programs and Books

Some of the seminars mentioned above are given over the weekend and incorporate a full Shabbos experience. Following are two additional programs and a sampling of books about Shabbos.

The National Jewish Outreach Programs (NJOP) has developed a program entitled "Turn Friday Night Into Shabbos." This is usually run by a member of the community (perhaps the Rabbi) and consists of candle-lighting, Friday evening services, and the Shabbos meal. It's the place where many people experience their first authentic Shabbos experience. Call 1-800-44 HEBRE(W).

♦ The National Council for Synagogue Youth (NCSY) runs Shabbatons throughout the country. Each branch is organized locally to meet the needs of the particular community. Call 212-563-4000.

♦ Many books have been written on the laws of Shabbos. One particularly good author is Rabbi Simcha Bunim Cohen, who has written a few masterpieces on these laws, including books on kiddush (*The Radiance of Shabbos*), warming food (*The Shabbos Kitchen*), and a number of the categories (*The Shabbos Home*). (Mesorah Publications)

♦ Rabbi Zecharya Fendel's *Seasons of Majesty* (the volume on Shabbos) is a wonderful collage of Shabbos law, outlook, and thought. Particularly inspirational is the chapter entitled

"Calling Shabbos a Delight."

♦ *Rest and Happiness* (*Minucha V'Simcha*), (Feldheim distributors) published by the Jewish Education Program, is a good book on Shabbos and Jewish holidays. Also, *Friday Night and Beyond* (Aronson Publishers) is replete with insights and stories that make Shabbos a real life experience. *The Taste of Shabbos: The Complete Sabbath Cookbook* is a perfect starting point for cooking the Shabbos meals. The Lubavitch women's cookbook entitled *Spice and Spirit*, also offers a unique perspective of the elevated role that food plays in Jewish life.

♦ Rabbi Aryeh Kaplan's booklet entitled *Sabbath-Day of Eternity* is a conversational discussion of Shabbos, written by a masterful author. The booklet is included in Volume Two of the *Anthology* (Mesorah Distributors).

♦ A candle-lighting hotline for the weekly times is available at 718-774-3000. The calculation is based on zip code and can be inaccurate by up to three minutes. For better accuracy, check sunset in your local newspaper and then subtract eighteen minutes. Shabbos is over on Saturday night at nightfall, which is approximately an hour and 10 minutes later than the time for candle-lighting.

Weekly Torah Thoughts

The best Torah thoughts are the result of diligent study presented from a personal perspective. Your own insights, remarks or stories are what make a presentation, formal or informal, a real success. Here are some starting points.

♦ The *Stone Chumash* (Bible) published by Artscroll has become a popular text for synagogues throughout America. This single volume contains the Five Books of Moses with a contemporary English translation, as well as an insightful commentary.

♦ The Judaica Press has an English-Hebrew translation of the Bible and the prophets. This series is ideal for in-depth study of the traditional commentaries.

♦ Rabbi Dr. A.J. Twerski's *Living Each Day* (Mesorah Publications) contains short thoughts for each day of the year. The book concludes with short essays for each of the weekly portions. As with all of his books, this book is both entertaining and stimulating, urging us on to the joys of spiritual growth.

♦ Rabbi Zelig Pliskin's *Growth through Torah* (Feldheim Distributors) is a great compilation of stories, insights, and general Jewish thought. Based on the weekly portion, this book is a big help for students and teachers alike.

♦ *The Pirkei Avos Treasury—Ethics of the Fathers* (Mesorah Publications) includes commentary and anecdotes to illuminate these sayings of our sages.

♦ *Parsha Parables,* by Rabbi Mordechai Kamenetzky (Feldheim Distributors) has a nice insight and story for each portion, throughout the year.

Prayer books

♦ The Artscroll *Siddur* (prayer book) stands out as a masterpiece of Jewish literature. It contains a contemporary English translation as well as an enlightening commentary. It has received nationwide acclaim as *the* prayer book for today's American Jew.

♦ NCSY has published *The NCSY Bencher* which contains a number of Shabbos prayers and songs, many of which are both translated and transliterated into English. A true plus for beginners, it's a great help in singing along even before you know the words.

♦ *The Companion Guide to the Shabbat Prayer Service* (The Judaica Press) by Moshe Sorcher is useful for the beginner's service. It includes selections from the prayers in transliterated form, as well as great stories for insightful reading.

Recommended Reading

♦ *Generation to Generation* (CIS Publishers), by Rabbi Dr. A.J. Twerski, is a book of recollections of the Rabbi's youth, growing up in a religious home. Rabbi Twerski's candor and beautiful insights make the book a must read for every Jew.

♦ *The Secret of Jewish Femininity* (Feldheim Distributors) by Tehilla Abramov, is an upbeat book about the role of the Jewish woman in marriage. Based on the laws of family purity, the book has become a best seller, as many Jews turn to Judaism to achieve stability in marriage.

♦ A follow-up book, *Two Halves of a Whole* (Feldheim Distributors), is written for both men and women. This book, written by Rabbi and Mrs. Abramov, provides humorous anecdotes and useful insights to strengthen a Jewish marriage. Their ideas are backed by the traditions of Israel, as well as years of counseling in this important field.

♦ *Candlelight* (Mesorah Publications) by Avi Shulman is a compilation of essays on life which are simple in presentation, invigorating in insights, and powerful in their message.

♦ Hanoch Teller's *Soul Series* contains wonderful, inspirational stories. Also recommended are his books *Above the Bottom Line,* and *Courtrooms of the Mind.*

For Children

♦ *The Best of Olomeinu* contains many inspirational stories about Shabbos and the Holidays.

♦ The Uncle Moishe music tapes make for good educational listening. Also, *Thirty-Six Jewish Songs* by Suki and Ding adapts classic children's tunes to educational words.

Charitable Organizations

Charity plays an important role in Jewish life. Although there are hundreds of wonderful charities, I include here two of my favorite.

♦ National Jewish Outreach Programs
   485 Fifth Avenue, Suite 701
   New York, NY 10017

NJOP is deeply committed to Jewish education throughout the United States. Their initial projects, including the Hebrew Reading Crash Course and Turn Friday Night Into Shabbos, have met with exceptional success.

♦ *Tomchei Shabbos* (Supporters of Shabbos) is an organization that ensures that poor families have a proper Shabbos meal. Boxes are delivered on Thursday night, in an anonymous and efficient manner.

Tomchei Shabbos volunteers are active in many Jewish communities. You may wish to inquire if such a program exists in your local community, either independently or as part of an existing organization.

Supporting such organizations is important, as the very nature of the Jewish people is to be charitable. As Maimonides so eloquently stated: "We have never seen or heard of a Jewish community that has not established charitable organizations. This is the legacy of our father Abraham, and it is in the merit of charity that we will be granted redemption."[1]

Shabbos Recipes

Matt's Chulent

- One pound flanken or rib meat
- One mid-sized onion
- One ounce oil
- 20 ounces water
- One-half cup barley
- One cup mixed beans (e.g., raw lima, pinto and northern beans)
- One teaspoon of: salt, paprika and garlic powder
- Two pinches of: onion powder and ground white pepper
- Two mid-size potatoes
- (Marrow bones for added flavor)

1) (Soak beans in water overnight, optional.) Boil barley in water for 35 minutes, drain.

2) Peel and dice onion thinly. Put a three quart pot on a low flame and put half of the ounce of oil into the pot. Add onion to pot and fry. Mix the onion so that it doesn't burn. If you need more liquid add a bit of oil or water as needed. (If you are making the chulent in a crockpot you can skip the frying process, and simply add the onion to the other ingredients in the next step.)

3) When onion is browned, add twenty ounces of water, spices and beans and bring the pot to a steady boil. Cut potatoes in half and add to pot. Barley goes in last. Make sure

everything is covered with water. Cover the pot and keep it at a full boil for a few minutes. Then lower the flame and keep it at a medium boil for two hours. The chulent is now ready. Lower the flame, but maintain a slow steady boil.

4) Before Shabbos, put a *blech* (metal covering) over the fire. Put the pot on the *blech* and adjust the fire to maintain a slow steady boil. Keep pot covered and leave cooking until Shabbos lunch. Enjoy!

This recipe is good for four generous portions. You can naturally adjust it to fit your needs. Chulent is one dish that can be experimented with. Ask around and discover the ingredients that you like most.

Pinny's Chulent

- ♦ 1/4 cup mixed beans
- ♦ 1/4 cup barley
- ♦ 1/4 cup brown sugar
- ♦ 2 squirts of ketchup
- ♦ 1 small onion, quartered
- ♦ 1 teaspoon salt
- ♦ 2 cloves of fresh garlic
- ♦ dash of pepper
- ♦ 5 cups water
- ♦ 5 large potatoes
- ♦ 1/2 pound chuck roast

Put ingredients in a covered pot or crockpot and boil for two hours. Your chulent is now ready to be placed on the *blech*. Adjust the fire to a slow steady boil and leave it there until Shabbos lunch. Makes five portions.

Rhine Challah

(Makes four large loaves)
- ♦ 5 pounds flour (plus some extra flour to put on the baking pans)
- ♦ 5 cups water, warm to touch
- ♦ 2 eggs
- ♦ 1 tablespoon salt
- ♦ 1/2 cup sugar
- ♦ 1 tablespoon oil
- ♦ 1 package dry yeast or a 1/2 ounce yeast cake
- ♦ Poppy or sesame seeds to sprinkle on loaves (optional)

1. Take one cup water and add yeast, together with a dash of sugar and a dash of salt to activate and cause foaming. Mix gently.

2. In a large mixing bowl place flour, sugar, salt, one egg, oil, and water. Add the yeast mixture.

3. Knead the dough very well. Pay attention to the consistency of the dough. If it is too sticky, put some flour on your fingers to make it easier to work with. If it is too tough, add very small amounts of warm water as you work. Wait a few minutes before adding more water.

4. When the dough is kneaded well (i.e., it has a smooth consistency, and no pockets of flour), cover it with a towel and let it rise for one hour. After one hour, punch it down and let it rise for a second hour. After the second hour punch it down again.

5. Now you are ready to take "challah." With all the dough together in the bowl, cover the dough with a towel, and before you take an olive size piece off recite the blessing: *Baruch Atah Ado-noy Elo-heinu Melech haolam asher kidishanu bimitvosov vitzivanu lihafrish challah.* (Blessed are You G-d, King of the universe Who sanctified us with the commandments and commanded us to separate challah.) If you are working with a recipe that has less than five pounds, do not make this blessing. Instead simply say: "This should be challah." (See pgs. 3-4 for more explanation on this procedure.)

6. Now you are ready to form the loaves. Flour two baking pans, and cut the dough into quarters. Braid each quarter into one loaf. To braid the dough, divide each quarter into three small sections and roll each section between your hands until you form a strand. Then take three strands and line them up side by side. Connect the three by pinching one end together. Now you are ready to braid. Take the braid furthest to the right side and bring it to the middle of the other two. Now take the left-most braid and bring it to the middle of the other two. Repeat this procedure (right-most braid to the middle, then left-most braid to the middle) until the loaf is fully braided. Pinch the ends together and repeat this procedure for the rest of the dough.

7. You should now have four braided loaves. Arrange them on the baking pans. Beat one egg and "paint" the loaves. If you wish, sprinkle the loaves with poppy or sesame seeds.

8. Place the two trays of loaves into the oven at 350 degrees for 35 minutes or until golden brown. (Reverse trays after 15 minutes so they will bake evenly.) Enjoy!

Questions and Answers

*J*uadism is an ongoing experience of growth and insight. The most significant sign of successful study is to walk away inspired and full of questions. Following are some questions that often come up.

Question: A woman normally begins Shabbos when she lights the Shabbos candles. Is there any way that she can begin Shabbos at a later time?

Answer: A woman may light candles on condition (i.e., that she is not accepting Shabbos at this time).[2] Instead, she will begin Shabbos at sundown, or earlier, if she is ready to do so.

The authorities prefer that this loophole should not be used regularly.[3] Whenever possible, the woman should accept the holiness of Shabbos when she lights the candles.

However, a man who lights Shabbos candles does not accept Shabbos at the time of lighting. Nevertheless, it is proper for him to have in mind that he is not accepting Shabbos at this time.[4]

Question: Is there any pattern to the way the Rabbis instituted their legislation to safeguard Shabbos?

Answer: Yes. Dayan Grunfeld explains (*The Sabbath*, page 33) that there are three subdivisions of Rabbinic legislation in the Shabbos. They are:

A) *Cases that outwardly resemble a forbidden act and could be confused with it.* This would refer to acts done destructively, but that nevertheless resemble one of the categories. Tearing a piece of paper for no apparent purpose, for example, is not forbidden by Torah law. It is prohibited by Rabbinic legislation because destructive tearing can easily be confused with constructive tearing (e.g., tearing a bad stitch in order to re-sew it properly).

B) *Acts normally linked with a forbidden action.* For example, purchasing an item since it is associated with writing to record the transaction. The Rabbis therefore legislated a prohibition against business dealings on Shabbos.

C) *An act that leads to a forbidden action.* For instance, it is forbidden to climb a tree on Shabbos since it is not unusual to break a twig while doing so. (See elaboration on pg. 165).

It is interesting that traditional Jews are sometimes called Rabbinic Jews. This is not derogatory. It is actually an expression of appreciation—we call ourselves by the name of the Rabbis in appreciation for their foresight in enacting safeguards that have protected the Shabbos for all time.

Question: I once heard that on Shabbos I shouldn't drag a heavy chair or bench on the ground because it may make a furrow. I was wondering why that would be a problem, considering that all of the categories require creative intent, and the intent here is clearly *not* to make a furrow.

Answer: Let me clarify this important point by saying that it is permitted to carry a chair over the ground while taking it from one place to another. Even though the chair might occasionally drag on the ground and dig a furrow, it is not the intended purpose of the action and is permitted.[5] If, however, the chair is particularly heavy, and will definitely create a furrow, then such an action would be forbidden.[6]

Our Rabbis base this law on a concept entitled *psik reisha*, and explain that even if there is no intent for the creativity, but that creativity is a direct and definite result of the action, then the action is forbidden. Therefore, in our case, it is not permitted to carry a particularly heavy chair or bench over the ground in a way that it will definitely drag on the ground. Even though there is no intent for the furrow that is created, since it is something that will definitely occur, it is included in the category of plowing (#1).

Question: You explained that it is permitted to move a kettle from one part of the *blech* to another. If I lifted the kettle off the *blech* can I return it?

Answer: With regard to liquids cooked before Shabbos, if the liquid is still warm,[7] it may be moved from one part of the *blech* to a warmer part; or, if it was removed from the *blech*, it may be returned, provided that the following conditions are met:

1. the item is fully cooked. 2. the item is *still* warm, and 3. there was intent to return it to the *blech* and the item was not put down.[8]

Question: Is it permissible to use hot tap water on Shabbos?

Answer: Hot tap water comes from the boiler which heats the water and then sends it through the pipes to the sink. As water is removed from the boiler, new, cold water is added. Thus, the removal of the hot water causes the new cold water to be cooked. In fact, the pressure that forces the hot water to the sink, is created by the addition of the cold water. For this reason, the authorities maintain that it is *not* permitted to use hot tap water on Shabbos.[9]

Question: Is there anything wrong with climbing a tree on Shabbos?

Answer: A Rabbinic legislation prohibits leaning on or making use of a tree. The Rabbis feared that if one were allowed to use or climb a tree, one might break off a branch for a different use, which violates the category of harvesting (#3).[10] For this reason one should not hang a jacket on the branch of a tree, nor climb a tree on Shabbos. Similarly, one should not lie down on a hammock that is tied directly to a tree.

It is, however, permitted to make use of the "side of the side" of the tree. This means that if the item being used (e.g., the hammock) is one level removed from the tree, then this Rabbinic legislation does not apply.[11] To illustrate: it is permitted to lie in a hammock that is *not* attached directly to the tree, but rather to hooks that are attached to the tree. Since the hammock is the "side of the side" of the tree (i.e., not directly attached to the tree, but rather one level removed from it) it is permitted to lie down in that hammock on Shabbos.

Question: When I spend Shabbos with observant friends,

I see them squeezing pieces of lemon on their fish. Is this permitted?

Answer: The prohibition of squeezing (#5) applies only if the fruit is squeezed to produce a drink. If, however, it is squeezed onto a food, then it is not included in this category.[12] Thus there is no problem with squeezing a lemon onto chicken or fish, since the juice never appears as a liquid, but is immediately joined with the solid. In such cases, the squeezing is deemed to be the separation of a solid from a solid, and not the forbidden act of producing juice.

Question: I find it difficult to understand which types of selecting (#7) are permitted, and which are prohibited. Can you clarify the rules of this category?

Answer: When considering sorting on Shabbos, ask yourself the following three questions to know if the selection is permitted or prohibited on Shabbos.

Question One: Are you choosing the desired item or are you removing the undesired item? The prohibition of selecting is when you remove the undesirable from the desirable to enhance the product.

For example, if there is a fruit arrangement on the table, you may take any item that you desire. Taking what you want is *not* considered selecting.

If, however, you were given a plate of pineapple with some cut up strawberry on top which you do not want, don't remove the strawberry pieces and put them aside. Instead, leave the undesired strawberry pieces in place, and simply eat the desired pineapple from around it.

Question Two: Are you selecting the desired item by hand or with a utensil? Selecting is forbidden when it is done with a utensil such as a sieve or slotted spoon.

For example, one may not pour noodle soup through a strainer to "select" the noodles from the soup.

It is, however, permitted to use a ladle to remove the desired matzoh balls from a pot of soup. In such a case, the spoon is deemed an extension of your hand. Its purpose is not to select more effectively, but rather so as not to get your hand dirty or wet.[13]

Question Three: Are you making the selection for immediate use? Even when taking something desirable with your hands, you can do so on Shabbos only if you will be using it immediately.

It is not necessary for the selection to be *literally*, for immediate use. For example, if you are preparing a meal, you may prepare all the courses of the meal beforehand. Therefore, for example, you can select the good strawberries from the bad for a dessert dish, even if the dessert won't be served until the end of the meal.[14]

Choosing your children's clothing the night before the clothing will be worn is not considered for immediate use, and is thus not permitted on Shabbos. If the clothes were mixed up in a laundry basket, you cannot sort them on Shabbos, even though you are taking the items that you want.[15]

It is therefore best to sort all clothes needed for Shabbos before Shabbos begins. If you didn't, on Shabbos you may lift away clothing that you do not want in order to reach the item that you want to wear. This should only be done immediately prior to the time that you want to wear the clothing.[16]

Question: If a person lives far away from a synagogue how can you forbid him from driving to synagogue on Shabbos?

Answer: Before we discuss the logistical and emotional aspects to this problem, let's analyze the question from an objective view of the laws we have discussed.

For a number of reasons, it is forbidden to drive a car on Shabbos. The most obvious is that the way a car works is through the combustion of fuel. That combustion, which generates the car's power, violates the laws against fueling a fire (#32). Additionally, the way a car is started and controlled is through various types of electronic devices (see #34). Finally, when the car door is opened, a light goes on, which violates the laws against turning on a light on Shabbos (#32).

Simply said, driving a car on Shabbos would not be in keeping with the sanctity of Shabbos. Nevertheless, the difficulty encountered in such a situation must be addressed. One option is to spend Shabbos in a Jewish community whenever possible. Those Jews who live in closer proximity to the synagogue can host their friends for Shabbos, and experience a memorable Shabbos of both friendship and sanctity. In fact, the legacy of our father Abraham is hospitality and is one of the vital signs of a vibrant Jewish community.[17]

The result of the prohibition against driving is that people walk to synagogue on Shabbos. Many people find the experience invigorating. It can be a wonderful opportunity to slow down from the quick-paced work week. If walking is not an option, consider praying at home. Although communal prayer has additional potency as well as social value, a private prayer is also accepted. Ultimately, we realize that it is worthwhile to sacrifice communal prayer for the sake of one's religious principles.

A side benefit of not driving to synagogue on Shabbos is that it encourages people to live within walking distance of the Jewish community. Being in close proximity of other Jews can be a source of inspiration and strength.

Incidentally, although walking on Shabbos is recommended, there are restrictions to going for a walk out of the city limits. Thus, in many suburban areas, it is best to consult an authority before going for a stroll out of the city limits. (This law is called *Techumin* and is discussed in Shulchan Aruch chapters 396-416.)

Question: When I travel through traditional Jewish neighborhoods I have noticed that many homes have special poles in their yards. What is the significance of those poles?

Answer: The poles that you saw are called an *eiruv*. As a result of those poles people are allowed to transfer (or carry) in the enclosed area. This concept of enclosure is discussed at length in a large tractate of the Talmud called *Eiruvin*. To understand the concept, allow me to begin with the background of the category of transfer (#39).[18]

From the Torah law there are three areas:

1. The public area, such as a street, which has many people passing through it.

2. The private area, designated and enclosed for private use. A house and a fenced-in yard are examples of this classifica-

tion. One is permitted to carry in these areas.

3. An area that does not fit into either of the previous categories, and is therefore not bound by their restrictions (e.g., a lake).

The laws of transfer state that one may not carry from a public area to a private area, or vice versa.[19] Thus we would not be allowed to carry something from our home into the street. Additionally, we cannot carry an object in the public area for a distance of four cubits (about six feet).[20]

Interestingly, most of what we would think of as a public area is really not, because many Rabbinical authorities rule that a true public area must have 600,000 people.[21] Instead, these areas fall into a fourth grouping, which is of Rabbinic origin. This grouping is called *"karmilis,"* a contraction of the two Hebrew words: *rach* (wet), and *mal* (dry).[22] This grouping of *karmilis* includes areas that are neither public nor private. Hence the comparison to being neither wet nor dry.

The significance of this fourth grouping is that when the Rabbis created it, they incorporated a loophole into their legislation. That is, they said that if the area in question is enclosed, then one may transfer in and out of this public area.[23] This is because the entire area is now classified as private. The type of enclosure that is used represents a door frame.[24] It has two posts, and a wire running above the posts. This simple representation of the door frame is repeated many times until the area in question has been enclosed. Building such an enclosure involves some intricate laws, and a competent authority should oversee its construction.

Endnotes

Introduction

1. Wouk, Herman, *This is My G-d*, pp.45-46 (reprinted with permission).
2. ibid., page 46.
3. Exodus 31:17.
4. Ethics of Our Fathers 4:1.
5. See also *Gateway to Happiness* by Rabbi Zelig Pliskin for further elaboration. In particular, the theme of Shabbos is discussed on pp.84-85.
6. See Talmud, Shabbos 130a.
7. Talmud, Shabbos 10b.
8. Deuteronomy 33:4.

Chapter 1 Preparing For The Queen

1. Talmud Avodah Zoroh, 3a.
2. The priests are known in Hebrew as *Kohanim*, or in the singular, *Kohein*. They are descendants of the first priest Aaron, the brother of Moses. The most well known honor given to priests is that a *Kohein* is called up first to the Torah reading.
3. Sefer HaChinuch 385. See Rabbeinu Bachya Numbers 15:20 where he compares the elevated status of the bread after this mitzvah is done to the miraculous manna which sustained the Jews in the desert. These laws are discussed in Shulchan Aruch, Yoreh Deah, Chapters 322-330.
4. Taamei Haminhagim 252.

Chapter 2 Candle-lighting

5. Proverbs 20:27. See also Talmud, Shabbos 32a, "The soul that I have placed in you is called a light."
6. For further elaboration of the role of a Jewish woman see Rabbi Yisroel Miller's *Guardian of Eden*, (Feldheim Publishers) as well as his essays in *What's Wrong With Being Happy?* (Mesorah Publications) entitled: Mrs. Rosenberg's Yeshiva and Devorah the Unknown.
7. The numerical value of *Chai*—which means life—is eighteen.
8. Shulchan Aruch 263:2-3
8a. Ramoh 263:5.
9. Ramoh 263:8, see also Mishnah Berurah note 37.

Chapter 3 The Source of Blessing

10. *Minucha V'Simchah* pp.35-36.
11. ibid., based on Medrash Bireishis Rabboh 11:8.
12. Based on *The Eye of a Needle* (Feldheim Publishers) pp.27-29.
13. Talmud, Sanhedrin 96a.
14. Based on a discussion that took place at a "Turn Friday Night Into Shabbos" Shabbos meal. Many thanks to the National Jewish Outreach Program for their innovative projects, as well as to Rabbi Aaron Gruman, whose insights have been incorporated in this book.
15. Machane Yisroel, Chapter Seven.

Chapter 4 Friday Night

16. See Talmud Shabbos 119b.
17. This song is taken from Proverbs 31:10-31.
18. Talmud, Pesachim 101a. See also Shulchan Aruch Chapter 273.
19. Shulchan Aruch Chapter 269.
20. Mishnah Berurah 269:1.
21. Pesachim 66a.
22. It is questionable if the Cantor truly has the public in mind when he makes this kiddush. He should be instructed to have everyone in mind, so that people can fulfill their obligation through his recital (Mishnah Berurah 273:30, and Shaar Tziyun note 34). See Mishnah Berurah 273:25. This practical application is cited in Taamei Haminhagim 278 note 1 in the name of Rabbi Yaakov of Marvege (c.1200, France).
23. Shulchan Aruch 272:2; Mishnah Berurah note 6. See Rabbi David Feinstein's *Kol Dodi Haggadah* (Mesorah Publications) 2:5,6 for how this measurement of ounces was derived from the original measurement given at Sinai. On a basic level we realize that if we must make kiddush on wine there must be a measurement as to how much is considered a significant, appropriate amount.
24. Talmud Brachos 35a. The reason we make a blessing before we eat anything is simple. When a human being gives you something, you say "Thank You." It follows that when G-d extends his hospitality to us, and allows us to benefit from His blessings, it is proper to say "Thank You." A blessing is our means of thanking G-d; it is simply a matter of proper social etiquette.
25. Ramoh 271:9 and Mishnah Berurah notes 45 and 46. See Aruch HaShulchan, Choshen Mishpat 17:1,5.
26. At least a cheekful of the Kiddush wine must be drunk (Shulchan Aruch

271:13). In the *Kol Dodi Haggadah* 2:9 Rabbi David Feinstein places a cheekful at 3/4 of an ounce. Others maintain that it is proper to drink a full two ounces. See Shulchan Aruch 271:14 and Mishnah Berurah 190:18.

27 Shimiras Shabbos Kihilchasoh 48:6.

28. Mishnah Berurah 271:5. See also Shimiras Shabbos Kihilchasoh 47:33 as well as Shulchan Aruch 589:9.

29. A similar concept can be found in Exodus 20:23, with regard to the honor of the Altar. See the commentary in Artscroll's Stone Chumash, based on Rashi.

30. See Talmud Chulin 106a.

31. Shulchan Aruch 159:1.

32. Mishnah Berurah 158:45 discusses the reason for washing each hand twice, as well as the importance of drying the hands afterwards. Shulchan Aruch 158:10 states that it is preferable to use a large cup and to pour liberally.

The hand-washing before meals differs from the hand-washing that we do in the morning when we wake up. The morning washing is three times on each hand, alternately. That is, once on the right, once on the left, once on the right etc. The morning washing is commonly understood to be of Kabbalistic origin and it infuses our hands with an invigorating spiritual force which assists us throughout the day. See Mishnah Berurah 4:1,10.

33. Three blessings were uttered by G-d during creation. The first was to fish, "be fruitful and multiply and fill the sea," the second to man, "be fruitful and multiply and fill the land," and the third to Shabbos, "And G-d blessed the seventh day and sanctified it." When a person eats fish on Shabbos he combines all three blessings. (Bnei Yissaschar, as quoted in *The Book of Shabbos* p.25).

34. See Rabbeinu Yonah, Pirkei Avos 1:12.

35. Rabbi Meir Simcha Hacohein of Divinsk, as quoted in *The Spero Bencher*.

36. An alternate explanation is that women rely on the opinion of Tosfos Eiruvin 17b that this washing is not required. See Ramoh 472:4 that it is possible for women to adopt a different custom than men.

Chapter 5 Shabbos Morning

37. See Mishnah Berurah 139:12,13.

Chapter 6 Shabbos Lunch

38. This expression is originally found in the Talmud, Yevamos 20a in a different context. The concept introduced here is based on the Chovos HaLivavos, Chapter Four where the author explains that all permissible actions can

actually be classified as mitzvohs, if they are done with the proper intentions. See also Kitzur Shulchan Aruch Chapter 31 for a further elaboration of this theme.

39. This theme is reiterated often in the writings of our Rabbis, based on the sentence (Proverbs 3:6) "In all of your endeavors you should know G-d." This means that a Jew remembers G-d even during his mundane affairs. In this way one's entire life becomes holy. See Rabbeinu Yonah's commentary to Ethics of Our Fathers 2:12, "And *all* of your actions should be for the sake of Heaven."

The great sage of our generation, Rabbi Moshe Feinstein (1895-1986), once asked a class of elementary school boys, "How does the Torah make you different than other people?" Initially the boys answered that because of the Torah they are obligated to learn Torah and keep the mitzvohs. Eventually Rabbi Feinstein guided them towards the insight that he had in mind. "Because you have Torah you act differently on the ball field. The game is played with good manners, and with honesty. We are not allowed to engage in name calling, or foul language. A Jew must behave properly...even on the ball field."

40. See Rabbeinu Bachya, Exodus 18:12.

41. Rambam 3:3; Shulchan Aruch Chapter 253.

42. See Ramoh Yoreh Deah 2:9.

43. See the Ramoh's concluding comments to Chapter 257. For additional mention about this divergent group see Rambam's commentary to Ethics of Our Fathers 1:3, and Ramoh Yoreh Deah 2:9.

46. Ramoh 257.

47. Based on an essay in *Between the Lines*, (Distributed by CIS Publishers) by Mrs. Anna Gotlieb, p.390.

48. Talmud Shabbos 55a.

49 See also Deuteronomy 28:47.

50. Koheles 7:8.

Chapter 7 Shabbos Afternoon

51. Based on Medrash Rabboh, Bamidbar 21:22.

Chapter 8 Spiritual Growth

52. Talmud, Shabbos 118b.

53. Kitzur Hilchos Shabbos, introduction.

54. Talmud Avodah Zorah 3a.

55. From the concluding portion of the daily morning prayers.

56. *Generation to Generation*, (CIS Publishers) p.131.

Endnotes

Chapter 9 Havdalah Farewell

57. Igros Moshe Volume 4 Chapter 62, as well as Yoreh Deah Volume 2 Chapter 79.

58. Shulchan Aruch 299:10, see Mishnah Berurah note 34.

59. Shulchan Aruch 296:1-2.

60. Psalms 23:5.

61. Talmud Eiruvin 65a.

62. Ramoh 296:1.

63. In Hebrew this added spiritual dimension is called the "Nishamah Yiseira," the extra soul. Mishnah Berurah 297:2.

64. Medrash Shocheir Tov, Chapter 92.

65. Noam Hashabbos p.43 based on Rabbeinu Bachya, Genesis 2:3.

66. Shulchan Aruch and Ramoh 296:2. Also see Shimiras Shabbos Kihilchasoh 60:1,5-7.

67. Ramoh 298:3.

68. Shulchan Aruch and Ramoh 296:8.

69. Transliterated from the Hebrew: Boruch Hamavdil Bein Kodesh LiChol.

70. Shulchan Aruch 299:10, Mishnah Berurah note 36.

71. See Shimiras Shabbos Kihilchasoh 63:8.

The Laws Of Shabbos

Introduction

1. Talmud Shabbos 33b.

2. Based on an insight from *The Eye of a Needle* (Feldheim Distributors) pp.29-30.

3. Talmud Avodah Zoroh 3a; Shimos Rabboh 34.

4. Based on *Around the Maggid's Table* by Rabbi Paysach Krohn, page 173.

Chapter 10 Jewish Law—the Basics

5. Introduction to *The Pentateuch* (The Judaica Press) by Rabbi Samson Raphael Hirsch.

6. See Ethics of Our Fathers 1:1.

7. Bier HaGolah Chapter 1.

8. See Rabbi Aaron Kotler's insight into the death of Rabbi Akivah's students, *Mishnas Rebbi Aaron* Volume 3, p.13.

9. Acharei Mos 73a.

10. See Rashi Deuteronomy 6:5.

Chapter 11 A Definition of Working

11. Ethics of Our Fathers 3:21.

12. The explanation of "physical-creativity" is based on the writings of Rabbi Samson Raphael Hirsch as explained by Dayan Grunfeld in *The Sabbath* (Feldheim Publishers).

13. Commentary to Exodus 25:2. See Medrash Tanchuma Pikudei Chapter 2.

14. This theme of imitating G-d's creation in the world is not limited to the building of the Sanctuary. Every day the Jew tries to imitate G-d's goodness in this world. For example: Just as G-d is merciful so we are told to be merciful. Interestingly, our good deeds are reciprocated in kind. "If you will hear the supplication of the poor man then G-d will hear your supplication." (See Ramoh, Yoreh Deah 247:3.)

15. In his exemplary overview of the day of Shabbos, Herman Wouk writes (*This is My G-d* p.51): The seven-day cycle is a seal that cuts very deep into Jewish life. All planning relates to the creation day: plans of work, of travel, of leisure, even of a place to live. Bulking so large in life, coming so often, the Sabbath has a lifetime in which to imprint its meanings on the spirit and the brain. Those who keep the day inevitably have the ideas of creation and the Creator, of the Exodus and of Jewish identity, strongly in mind.

16 See Nefesh HaChaim 1:4.

Chapter 12 Thirty-nine Categories—Gardening

17. Shulchan Aruch 336:7, Mishnah Berurah note 41.

18. Mileches Shabbos; Shimiras Shabbos Kihilchasoh 26:24.

Chapter 13 Food Preparation

19. Kitzur Hilchos Shabbos 11; Mishnah Berurah 319:24.

20. Shulchan Aruch 321:12 and Mishnah Berurah note 45; see Shimiras Shabbos Kihilchasoh 6:6.

21. Igros Moshe Volume 4, Chapter 74:3.

22. Shulchan Aruch 319:10.

23. Shimiras Shabbos Kihilchasoh 8:25.

24. Shulchan Aruch 321:16, see also Mileches Shabbos p.88 as well as Igros Moshe Volume 4, Chapter 74. A thorough discussion of this matter can be found in *Children in Halachah* pp.96-100.

25. Igros Moshe Volume 4, Chapter 74:3 maintains that 110 degrees is considered hot enough to cook.

26. Shulchan Aruch 318:11.

27. Igros Moshe Volume 1, Chapter 93.
28. Shulchan Aruch 318:4. See Biur Halacha 253:3.
29. Ramoh 318:15.
30. See Igros Moshe Volume 4, Chapter 74:15,16.

Chapter 14 Cloth Production

31. See Rashi Exodus 26:1.
32. See Rashi Shabbos 31a.
33. Mishnah Berurah 303:85.
34. Shulchan Aruch 303:27.
35. Aruch Hashulchan 327:4; Shimiras Shabbos Kihilchasoh 15:37.
36. Shulchan Aruch 303:25.
37. In *Contemporary Halakhic Problems* Volume 4 Rabbi J. David Bleich makes a strong case against the use of Shabbos makeup. See pp.113-119.
38. Shulchan Aruch 320:19, Mishnah Berurah note 56.
39. *The Book of Shabbos* p.180.

Chapter 15 Leather Production

40. Rashi Exodus 25:5 and Rashi's commentary to the Talmud Shabbos 73a. Rabbi Samson Raphael Hirsch 26:14. Another source for the unicorn can be found in Talmud Shabbos 28b.
41. Mishnah Berurah 316:18.
42. Chayei Adom 30:4.
43. Rambam 11:1.
44. Shulchan Aruch 316:8. *The Sabbath,* page 45.
45. Shulchan Aruch 321:2.
46. Ramoh 326:10 and Mishnah Berurah note 30. See *The Book of Shabbos* p.219.
47. See *Children in Halacha*, pp.90-93 and note 70.
48. Mileches Shabbos p.255; Shimiras Shabbos Kihilchasoh 11:15.
49. Shimiras Shabbos Kihilchasoh 23:16.
50. Mishnah Berurah 340:41.
51. Shimiras Shabbos Kihilchasoh 23:16. Also, see *The Shabbos Home,* pp.97-98.

Chapter 16 Miscellaneous Categories

52. Ramoh 317:1; Mishnah Berurah note 7.
53. Mishnah Berurah 317:23. *The Book of Shabbos* p.191; Kitzur Hilchos Shabbos p.65; *The Shabbos Home* pp.213-214.

54. *The Sabbath* p.45.

55. Igros Moshe Volume 2, Chapter 84 and Volume 4, Chapter 186; Mishnah Berurah 340:29; *The Book of Shabbos* p.195.

56. Mishnah Berurah 340:45.

57. *The Shabbos Home* Volume 1, pp.84-85. See also Mileches Shabbos for a thorough explanation of these laws.

58. Shimiras Shabbos Kihilchasoh 9:1-3. See also Igros Moshe Volume 1, Chapter 122.

59. Shimiras Shabbos Kihilchasoh 9:8, see note 31.

60. Shimiras Shabbos Kihilchasoh 9:12. In note 48 the opinion of Rabbi S.Z. Auerbach is quoted, that one may tear in between the letters, as long as an actual letter is not torn apart.

61. Rabbi S.Z. Auerbach in Meorei Eish Chapter 3, pp.112-113.

62. Shimiras Shabbos Kihilchasoh 13:23.

63. Ramoh 334:26; Mishnah Berurah 278:3.

64. Ramoh 334:26 and Mishnah Berurah note 73; Shimiras Shabbos Kihilchasoh 41:1-2 and note 7.

65. Mishnah Berurah 317:16,18; Shimiras Shabbos Kihilchasoh 15:60.

66. Shimiras Shabbos Kihilchasoh 13:1, note 1. Kitzur Hilchos Shabbos 38:2.

Chapter 17 Erecting the Sanctuary

67. See Rabbi Samson Raphael Hirsch, Numbers 9:16-23.

68. Mileches Shabbos p.260. This is in addition to the general prohibition against using electricity (see category #34).

69. See Kihilas Yaakov of Rabbi Yaakov Yisroel Kanievsky ("The Steipler") in his essay to Talmud Shabbos 75b.

70. Mishnah Berurah 340:17. Shimiras Shabbos Kihilchasoh 9:12.

71. Mishnah Berurah 340:15

72. Ramoh 340:3. Mishnah Berurah note 17 rules that it is permissible to bite into the letters. See also Shimiras Shabbos Kihilchasoh 11:7.

73. Many authors translate this category as "carrying," and that is the way it is known in the Jewish world. I have chosen the word "transfer" because this definition makes it easier to understand the nature of this category. The category refers to an act that transfers an object from the private domain to the public, or vice versa. Also included in this category is the act of carrying an object more than four cubits (about six feet) in the public domain. This case is based on the idea that the place of an object is the area in which it is. When one carries the object from its place of resting, he has transferred it out of its original location. See Mishnah Berurah 349:1.

74. Shulchan Aruch Chapter 346.

75. See Shulchan Aruch and Ramoh 303:18.

76. *The Sabbath*, page 28.

77. Heard from Rabbi Shaya Cohen at an Arachim Seminar in Lakewood N.J., January 1996.

Chapter 18 Muktza

78. Bais Yosef Chapter 308.

79. This topic was addressed beautifully in an article by Rabbi Yisroel Rackowsky, *Jewish Observer* September 1993.

80. Rambam 24:12.

81. For a more complete discussion of these laws and their applications, see Rabbi Bodner's *The Halachos of Muktza*.

82. Shulchan Aruch 308:4.

83. Shulchan Aruch 308:3.

84. Shulchan Aruch 308:38.

85. Shulchan Aruch 310:7

86. Shulchan Aruch 310:8. See Mishnah Berurah note 33 where he states that equal value is not sufficient to rule with leniency on the base. See also Shimiras Shabbos Kihilchasoh 20:55.

87. Shulchan Aruch 308:22.

88. The type of muktza that is involved here is very stringent. This type of muktza would not be allowed to be moved for any reason, because when Shabbos began the candles were burning. At that time the candelabra could not be moved for fear of extinguishing the candles. If the table was classified as a base, it would not be able to be moved for any reason.

89. See Igros Moshe Volume 3, Chapter 51.

90. Igros Moshe Volume 4, Chapter 91:5. See Shimiras Shabbos Kihilchasoh Chapter 28, note 54.

91. Ramoh 308:6.

92. Shulchan Aruch 311:8. Shimiras Shabbos Kihilchasoh 22:34, and note 86.

93. *In the Footsteps of the Maggid*, p.116.

Chapter 19 On Jewish Continuity

94. Deuteronomy 30:15,19.

Chapter 21 Opportunities for Study

1. Matnos Aniyim 9:3 and 10:1.

Question and Answer Section

2. Ramoh 263:10.

3. Mishnah Berurah 263:44.

4. Mishnah Berurah 263:42.

5. Shulchan Aruch 337:1.

6. Mishnah Berurah 337:4.

7. Ramoh 318:15.

8. Shulchan Aruch 253:2; Shimiras Shabbos Kihilchasoh 1:18-19. Preferably both conditions in item three should be met. In cases of need either condition is sufficient.

9. Shimiras Shabbos Kihilchasoh 1:39.

10. Shulchan Aruch 336:1, Mishnah Berurah note 1.

11. Shulchan Aruch 336:13, see also Mishnah Berurah note 59.

12. Shulchan Aruch 320:4.

13. Igros Moshe Volume 1, Chapter 124; Shimiras Shabbos Kihilchasoh 3:45.

14. Ramoh 319:1; Shimiras Shabbos Kihilchasoh 3:63.

15. Shimiras Shabbos Kihilchasoh 3:68.

16. Shimiras Shabbos Kihilchasoh 15:42, based on Biur Halacha to 319:3.

17. See Genesis 18:2-8 where the hospitality of Abraham is described. Tradition teaches that Abraham's tent had an opening on each side, so as to welcome travellers to partake in his hospitality.

18. Based on the Talmud Shabbos 9a; see also the introduction of the Mishnah Berurah to Chapter 345.

19. Shulchan Aruch 346:1.

20. See Shulchan Aruch 349:1.

21. This is the number of people that were recorded to have been in the desert after the Exodus from Egypt. See Shulchan Aruch 345:7; Tosfos Eiruvin 6a.

22. Shulchan Aruch 345:1.

23. Ramoh 363:26.

24. ibid.

Glossary

Amidah (or Shemoneh Esrei)—The most important prayer; said while standing in silent devotion.

Av—The fifth Hebrew month, usually corresponds to July and August. In this month the first and second Temples were destroyed.

Bar Mitzvah—When a boy becomes thirteen years of age and is considered a legal adult in Jewish law.

Bat Mitzvah—When a girl becomes twelve years of age and is considered a legal adult in Jewish law.

Blech—a sheet of metal used to cover the stove during Shabbos.

Bracha—blessing.

Challah—The piece of dough that is removed before forming the dough into loaves. In contemporary times, the word challah (pl. challohs) is usually used to refer to the Shabbos bread.

Cheshvan—The eighth month on the Jewish calendar.

Dayan—title of a Jewish judge, similar to the title "Rabbi."

DiRabbanan—A Rabbinic prohibition.

Dvar Torah—Torah thought.

Havdalah—the prayer said over wine at the conclusion of Shabbos.

Hermandad—Spanish secret police during the Inquisition.

Kabbalah—Jewish mystical and spiritual traditions.

Kallah—bride; commonly used to refer to a woman who is engaged.

Kiddush—the prayer said on Shabbos proclaiming the sanctity of the day.

Kosher—food fit for Jewish consumption according to religious law.

Lecho Dodi—a song which is sung during the Friday evening service.

Manna—holy food which miraculously sustained the Jewish people during their forty year sojourn in the desert.

Medrash—a record of oral traditions and homiletic thought, complementing the Talmud.

Melacha—An act of physical-creativity forbidden on Shabbos. The Talmud groups these acts into thirty-nine categories.

Mitzvah (pl. Mitzvohs)—commandment; commonly used to refer to any good deed.

Muktza—objects not intended for Shabbos use.

Oral Law—the part of Jewish tradition given orally to Moses at Sinai. Later, much of these teachings were recorded in the Talmud and in other books of Jewish scholarship.

Psik Reisha—An act which will definitely result in physical-creativity. Such action is prohibited on Shabbos even though the forbidden result was not intended. Example: dragging a heavy bench on the soil. Even though there is no intent to dig a furrow, since it will definitely occur it is included in plowing (#1).

Rav—Rabbi; title used for sages of the talmudic era.

Rabbeinu—Rabbi; title used for early commentators.

Rebbe—teacher of religious studies.

Rosh Yeshiva (pl. Roshei Yeshiva)—Dean of a yeshiva.

Sanctuary—The predecessor of the holy Temple in Jerusalem; built in a makeshift form and used during the forty year sojourn in the desert. Also known as Tabernacle, or in Hebrew *Mishkan.*

Savtie—grandmother.

Shabbos (pl. Shabbosos)—Sabbath.

Shalishudis—A slurred form of "Shalosh Seudos," or "three meals." This term refers to the third meal of Shabbos through which we complete the mitzvah to have three meals on Shabbos.

Shinuy—Doing an act of physical-creativity in an unusual manner. Such an act is usually Rabbinically prohibited. There are cases of great need where the Rabbinic prohibition is not applicable and doing the act in an unusual manner is permitted.

Shkiya—sunset; at this time Shabbos begins.

Siddur—prayer book.

Talmud—the somewhat informal record of the oral law. It is comprised of some five thousand pages, and is considered the mainstay of Jewish scholarship.

Tefilin—phylacteries; worn by religious men on weekdays. One box is placed on the arm facing the heart, to symbolize the dedication of our hearts to G-d. The second box is placed on the head to symbolize the dedication of our minds to religious life.

Temple—The final, permanent form of the Sanctuary as it was built by King Solomon in Jerusalem.

Torah—the lessons and laws received by the Jewish people at the revelation at Sinai. Includes the Bible, its commentaries, as well as the oral law.

Tractate—An individual volume of the Talmud.

Tzeis—nightfall; earliest time that Shabbos can be over. In the United States, fifty minutes after sunset.

Written Law—The five books of Moses; also includes an additional nineteen books written by the prophets with divine inspiration.

Yeshiva (pl. yeshivohs)—school for Jewish children which incorporates both religious and academic studies in the curriculum. On an advanced level, a yeshiva is devoted entirely to advanced religious studies.

Zeide—grandfather.

Zohar—The standard text for advanced Kabbalistic study.

Index

act of completion, 126-127
alarm clock, 138
apple picking on Shabbos, 101
appliances, use on Shabbos, 121,
    126-127, 145
ark, 39, 41, 93
aron, 41, 93
arranging the threads for the weaving
    process, 114
Auerbach, Rabbi Shlomo Zalman,
    88-89
baby food, 107
baking, 108
    challah, 3-4, 160-161
Bar/Bat Mitzvah, 43
bathroom tissue, 119-120
Berdichev, Rabbi Levi Yitzchok, 89
bimah, 38
birthday cake, 130
Betzalel, 92
blech, 108-109, 159, 164
blessings
    candle-lighting, 9
    bread, 28
    hand-washing, 28
    on wine, 24-26
    taking "challah," 4
    Torah reading, 39-40
    blessing the children, 20
blood, giving on Shabbos, 117
botei nirin, 114
building, 130-131
business, 55, 129, 134, 163
bread: see challah
broken glass, 139
Candle-lighting, 6-11, 153

how to do it, 8-9
quick facts, 10
time to do it, 9-10, 153
men, 10, 162
women, 7, 9, 10, 162
Cantor, 21-22,
car, using on Shabbos, 168-169
carrying, 131-132, 169-170
categories: see thirty-nine categories
chaff, 104-105
chair, dragging on soil, 163-164
challah, challohs, 3-4, 26-27, 28-29
    recipe, 160-161
charity, 59, 156-157
children, 1, 6-8, 13, 14, 20, 21-22, 29,
    30, 83, 140, 143, 167
Chofetz Chaim, 17, 87
chulent, 48-51, 108, 137
    recipes, 158-161
coffee, making on Shabbos, 110
combing raw materials, 112
cookbooks, 153
cooking, 108-110, 121, 164-165
crockpot, 137
covering the bread during kiddush,
    26-27
cream, applying on Shabbos, 118
crocheting, 114
customs, 21-22, 23-24, 49, 73
curtains in the Sanctuary, 111
danger, 126, 139
demolishing, 131
dyeing, 113
eating before Shabbos, 2
eiruv, 132, 169-170
Eishes Chayil, 19

electric mixer, 127
electricity, 124-127
electronics, 126-127, 145
Elijah the prophet, 76
Epstein, Rabbi Yechiel Michel of Novardok, 2
erasing, 130
erecting the Sanctuary, 92-93,ß 128-131
Ethics of our Fathers, 60-61, 154
extinguishing a fire, 125, 127
extra soul, 72
Feinstein, Rabbi Moshe, 88
filtering water on Shabbos, 107
fire, 94, 108-109, 124-127, 168
fish, 29, 31, 117, 122
fixing the threads during the weaving process, 114
flowers, 2, 101-102
food preparation, 100, 103-110
Friday afternoon, 2, 137
Friday evening, 6-7, 12, 17,
Friday night, 19-35, 72
fruit,
    gathering on Shabbos, 101
    picking on Shabbos, 101
    squeezing on Shabbos, 104
frying, 108
Gabbai, 38
gardening, 100-102
golden calf, 96
Grace after meals, 34-35, 43
grinding, 106
Grunfeld, Dayan, 85, 162
Hagofen, 24-25
haircuts, 112
halacha, 49
hand-washing, 27-28, 43
harvesting, 101

havdalah, 70-76
    text, 74
Hirsch, Rabbi Samson Raphael, 85
hot water, 100, 108, 110, 164-165
honesty, 55
honors in the synagogue, 38-39
hot food, 108-109
Jewish continuity, 142-144
Jewish education, 8, 143-144, 147-148, 156
Jewish law, 85-91
Kagan, Rabbi Yisroel Meir: see Chofetz Chaim
karmilis, 170
kiddush,
    day, 43-44
    night, 23-26
    quick facts, 26
killing insects, 117
kindling a fire, 124
King David, 62-63
kneading, 107, 117
knot, 122
kosher, 49, 71
Kotzk, Rabbi Menachem Mendel of, 19
laundering, 104, 112
leather production, 116-120
Lecho Dodi, 12-18
lipstick, 113
Maharal, 86
makeup, 113
making bundles, 101-102
marking, 119
matriarchs, 7, 20
menorah, 92
miscellaneous categories, 121-127
Mishnah Berurah, 87
molid, 118

moments after Shabbos, 76
Muktza, 134-141
Nehemiah, 135
Nevuchadnetzar, 16
nightfall, 70, 153
oneg, 60
oral law, 48, 49, 85
packages, opening on Shabbos, 124
painting, 113, 129
paper towels, 119
parchment, 116
Passover, 89-91
persistence, 56-57
physical-creativity, 93-95, 103, 121,
   132
Pirkei Avos, 60-61, 154
plants, watering on Shabbos, 101
plowing, 100
polishing shoes, 113
prayer, 7, 11, 36-38, 54-55, 61, 70, 80
   communal, 36
private area, 131, 169-170
prohibited actions, 86, 98-132
public area, 131, 169, 170
Rabbinic prohibitions, 86, 107, 109,
   125, 130, 137-138
Rabbinic safeguards, 86, 162-163
relationships,
   with G-d, 12, 26, 64, 87-89, 91, 95,
     103-104, 111, 118-119
   with family, 1, 13-14, 29, 60, 96,
     146
   with Shabbos, 1, 12, 15-16
rest, 16, 23, 44, 62, 68
returning food to blech, 109, 164
reward and punishment, 89
safeguards to Shabbos observance:
see Rabbinic safeguards
Sanctuary, 92-97

salt, 5, 29, 117
sanctify G-d's name, 46-47
scraping, 118
seeding, 101
selecting, 105
   by hand, 105, 167
   for immediate consumption, 105,
     167
   undesired from desired, 106, 166
sewing, 123
Shabbos afternoon, 43-44, 60-66
Shabbos meal, 2, 5, 17, 21, 24, 47
Shabbos perspectives,
   appreciating G-d's blessings, 34, 71
   as an investment, 14, 18
   as a source of blessing, 12-18, 104
   a sign, 17
   food, 3, 29-30
   joy of, 6, 56, 83-84
   life, 7, 13, 46-47, 54, 63, 67
   spirituality, 8, 46, 57-58, 67, 70,
     72, 82, 95-96, 130, 145
Shabbos preparations, 1
Shabbos Queen, 1, 12
Shabbos songs
   Koh Ribon, 32-34
   Minucha Visimcha, 31-32
   Mizmor LiDovid, 63-64
   Yidid Nefesh, 64
   Yom Zeh Michubod, 51-52
Shabbos stories, 6, 8, 13, 14-15,
   47, 50, 62, 68
Shalom Aleichem, 19
Shalosh Seudos, 61-62
shearing, 112
sifting, 107
skinning, 117
slaughter, 117
soap, 118

sorting, 105, 166-167
spices, 70-75
spinning, 113
spiritual-creativity, 132
squeezing, 104, 166
sunset, sundown, 6, 9-10, 151, 153, 162
synagogue, 2, 17, 19, 21-22, 36-37, 168
  words you may hear, 41-42
synagogue kiddush, 21-23
table, setting the, 4-5
talis, 37, 39
tanning, 117
tea, making on Shabbos, 110, 113
tearing 120, 122-124
technology, 121
telephone, 97, 126
Ten Commandments, 98
thirty-nine categories, 98-133
tissues, 119-120
Torah
  blessings on, 39-40
  Torah prohibitions, 48-49, 86, 101, 107, 118, 125
  Torah portion, 2, 30, 36
  Torah study, 61, 79
  Torah thoughts, 30, 43, 47, 53, 59
  How to do it, 39-40
trapping, 116
transfer, 131-132
tree,
  climbing, 163, 165
  pruning, 101
unicorn, 116
vegetables,
  cutting thinly, 106
  gathering on Shabbos, 101-102
  picking on Shabbos, 101

warming food, 108
warming water ,108
washing cup, 27
washing hands, 27-28
watering plants, 101
weaving, 111, 113-114
wine or grape juice, 4, 21, 23, 27, 70, 71, 73
winnowing, 104-105
women, 6, 9-11, 26, 34, 36-37, 73
wool, processing of, 111-113
work, 92-97
writing, 121, 124, 128-130
zemiros, 30

Bibliography

Abramov, Tehilla. *The Secret of Jewish Femininity*, Michigan: Targum Press, 1988.

Auerbach, Shlomo Zalman. *Meorei Eish*, Jerusalem: Bais Medrash Halachah—Moriah, 1980.

Bleich, J. David. *Contemporary Halakhic Problems Volume 4*, NY: Yeshiva University Press, 1995.

Bodner, Yisroel Pinchos. *The Halachos of Muktza*, New Jersey: Halacha Publications, 1981.

Chait, Baruch. *The 39 Avoth Melacha of Shabbath*, Israel: 1992.

Cohen, Simcha Bunim. *Children in Halacha*, New York: Mesorah Publications Ltd., 1993.

Cohen, Simcha Bunim. *The Radiance of Shabbos*, New York: Mesorah Publications Ltd., 1991.

Cohen, Simcha Bunim. *The Shabbos Home, Volume 1*, New York: Mesorah Publications Ltd., 1995.

Cohen, Simcha Bunim. *The Shabbos Kitchen*, New York: Mesorah Publications Ltd., 1996.

Coopersmith, Yitzchak. *The Eye of a Needle*, New York: Feldheim Publishers, 1993.

Eider, Shimon, *The Laws of Shabbos*, New York: Feldheim Publishers, 1970.

Feinstein, David. *The Kol Dodi Haggadah*, New York: Mesorah Publications Ltd., 1990.

Feinstein, Moshe. *Igros Moshe*, New York: Moriah Offset Co., 1959.

Gotlieb, Anna. *Between the Lines*, New Jersey: Bristol, Rhein & Englander, 1992.

Ganzfried, Shlomo. *Kitzur Shulchan Aruch*.

Goldwurm, Hersh. *The Early Acharonim*, New York: Mesorah Publications Ltd., 1989.

Greenberger, Shmuel. *Noam HaShabbos*, Bnei Brak, Israel: 1994.

Grunfeld, I. Introduction to *The Pentateuch*, by Rabbi Samson Raphael Hirsch. Rendered into English by Isaac Levy. Gateshead: Judaica Press Ltd., 1982.

Grunfeld, I. *The Sabbath*, Israel: Feldheim Publishers, 1954.

Hirsch, Samson Raphael. *Collected Writings Volume 3*, New York: Feldheim Publishers Ltd., 1984.

Kagan, Yisroel Meir HaCohen. *Mishnah Berurah*. (Available in an English translation through Feldheim Publishers.)

Kaplan, Aryeh. *Anthology, Volumes 1-2*, New York: Mesorah Publications Ltd., 1994.

Kaplan, Aryeh. *Encounters*, New York: Moznayim, 1990.

Katz, Mordechai. *Minucha ViSimcha*, New York: JEP Publications, 1982.

Kotler, Aaron. *Mishnas Rebbi Aaron*, New Jersey: 1988.

Krohn, Paysach J. *Around the Maggid's Table*, New York: Mesorah Publications Ltd., 1989.

Krohn, Paysach J. *In the Footsteps of the Maggid*, New York: Mesorah Publications Ltd., 1992.

Lieber, Moshe. *The Pirkei Avos Treasury*, New York: Mesorah Publications Ltd., 1995.

Miller, Yisroel. *What's Wrong With Being Human?*, New York: Mesorah Publications, 1992.

Miller, Yisroel. *What's Wrong With Being Happy?*, New York: Mesorah Publications, 1994.

Neuwirth, Yeshaya. *Shimiras Shabbos Kihilchasoh*, Jerusalem: Bais Medrash Halachah—Moriah, 1979. (Available in an English translation through Feldheim Publishers.)

Olomeinu—Our World, Torah Umesorah Publications.

Palatnik, Lori. *Friday Night and Beyond*, New Jersey: Jason Aronson Inc., 1994.

Pliskin, Zelig. *Gateway to Happiness*, New Jersey: Gross Bros. Printing Co. Inc., 1983.

Posen, J. *Kitzur Hilchos Shabbos*, Feldheim Publishers, 1984.

Scherman, Nosson. *The Complete Artscroll Siddur*, New York: Mesorah Publications Ltd., 1984.

Scherman, Nosson. *The Family Zemiros*, New York: Mesorah Publications Ltd., 1981.

Schwartz, Yoel. *The Man of Truth and Peace (Rabbeinu Shlomo Zalman Auerbach ztl)*, Israel: Feldheim Publishers Ltd. 1996.

Shtern, Yechiel Michel. *The Book of Shabbos*, Jerusalem 1996.

Sperling, Avraham Yitzchak. *Taamei Haminhagim Umikorei Hadinim*, Jerusalem: Eshkol, 1982.

Spero, Shubert and Moshe Halevi. *The Spero Bencher*, Cleveland: The Spero Foundation.

Stern, Yechiel Michel. *Mileches Shabbos*, Jerusalem 1994.

Teich, Shmuel and Goldwurm, Hersh. *The Rishonim*, New York: Mesorah Publications Ltd., 1982.

Twerski, Abraham J. *Generation to Generation*, New York: CIS Publishers, 1991.

Wein, Berel. *Echoes of Glory*, New York: Shaar Press, 1995.

Wein, Berel. *Herald of Destiny*, New York: Shaar Press, 1993.

Wein, Berel. *Triumph of Survival*, New York: Shaar Press, 1990.

Winston, Pinchas. *The "Y" Factor*, Ontario, Canada: Mercava Productions, 1993.

Wouk, Herman. *This is my G-d*, Boston: Little, Brown and Company, 1987.

Yoshor, Moses M. *The Chafetz Chaim*, New York: Mesorah Publications Ltd., 1984.